SUCCESS
DYNAMITE

SUCCESS DYNAMITE

DALE CARNEGIE
Public Speaking to Win!

A.H.Z. CARR
How to Attract Good Luck

THERON Q. DUMONT
The Power of Concentration

ABRIDGED AND INTRODUCED BY
MITCH HOROWITZ

Published by Gildan Media LLC
aka G&D Media.
www.GandDmedia.com

Public Speaking to Win! was originally published in 1926 as
Public Speaking: A Practical Course for Business Men
How to Attract Good Luck was originally published in 1952
The Power of Concentration was originally published in 1916
G&D Media Condensed Classics edition published 2018
Abridgement and Introduction copyright © 2015, 2018 by
Mitch Horowitz

FIRST EDITION: 2018

Cover design by David Rheinhardt of Pyrographx

Interior design by Meghan Day Healey of Story Horse, LLC.

ISBN: 978-1-7225-0091-7

Contents

Introduction

Unconventional Advice, Timeless Wisdom
By Mitch Horowitz

*S*uccess Dynamite features a remarkable and unusual range of self-development ideas within a very concise space. The value of these condensations—*Public Speaking to Win!*, *How to Attract Good Luck*, and *The Power of Concentration*—is that each one teaches vital lessons that are mostly overlooked in other success guides.

A case in point is Dale Carnegie's *Public Speaking to Win*! Carnegie, author of the legendary *How to Win Friends and Influence People*, actually began his career, and dedicated much of it, to teaching pubic speaking. In the years immediately before World War I, Carnegie—then spelled less elegantly as *Carnagey*—grasped that the new century was an age of communication. Anyone who wanted to succeed, in any field, the ex-actor reasoned, had to get across his ideas clearly, persuasively, and simply. This, he argued, was the key to distinction it every field from salesmanship to politics to teaching, and beyond.

In 1926, Carnegie assembled his principles into first book, abridged here to its essentials. The master speaker's lessons on how to grab and hold people's attention remain as relevant in our digital age as they were in his industrial one. I have delivered hundreds of public talks, at museums, universities, libraries and spiritual centers, and I have never encountered a guide that surpasses or even nears Carnegie's. He covers the basics of preparedness (the vital ingredient of every good talk), persuasiveness (you must be specific!), and the importance of passion (audiences smell fakery).

Another offbeat but vital addition to this collection is A.H.Z. Carr's *How to Attract Good Luck*. At first glance, the book sounds like a guide to gambling or getting something for nothing. It is anything but. Carr, a diplomat and economist who served in the administrations of Franklin Roosevelt and Harry Truman, was a dedicated student of human nature. He carefully observed the rise and fall of aspiring politicians, soldiers, and businessmen. Carr discovered that life actually provides us with definite opportunities to bend our luck in positive or negative directions. Good luck, in short, can be cultivated. Egotism, brashness, boredom, and dishonesty are generally unlucky, often in ways that are unexpected. By contrast, helping strangers, avoiding coarse company, and keeping away from people and situations that foster insecurity and extreme competitiveness wield a positive pull upward on our luck, and actually make a difference at critical and surprising moments.

Finally, this anthology includes an abridgement of *The Power of Concentration* by Theron Q. Dumont, the pseudonym of New Thought writer and publisher William Walker Atkinson. Atkinson is best known for another book that he wrote also pseudonymously: the occult classic, *The Kybalion*. Under his byline as Theron Q. Dumont, Atkinson, in what is one of his finest works, provides ideas about "rewiring" your brain that didn't become popular until the revolutions in cognitive therapy and neuroplasticity generations after he published this book in 1916. But *The Power of Concentration* retains more than its relevance. It conveys something about the dynamism and epic possibility of the human spirit, which is absent from most of today's therapeutic guides. In my view, it is one of the most powerful New Thought books ever written.

Napoleon Hill once noted the importance of *contrasting favorably* with your competitors. *Success Dynamite* gives you the very formulas to help you stand out. Its ideas are powerful and workable but *neglected*. Hence, they give you an edge. Take in these books carefully, and you will stand out from the others in line.

PUBLIC SPEAKING TO WIN!

PUBLIC
SPEAKING
TO WIN!

by Dale Carnegie

The Original Formula to
Speaking with Power

Abridged and Introduced
by Mitch Horowitz

THE CONDENSED [logo] CLASSICS LIBRARY™

Contents

The Power of What You Say

Nearly everything worth accomplishing in life comes down to communication. Your ability to sway others, win support, gain resources, succeed in your work, and correct injustice rests on your power of persuasion.

Even in our social-media age, the spoken word remains paramount. Candidates are elected because of what they say and how. Court trials hang on spoken testimony. Job interviews are face-to-face encounters. The same holds true for pitches to clients, donors, investors, customers, and financial backers. If you are seeking a career as a teacher, military officer, actor, broadcaster, or leader in any almost any field, your speaking ability is vital to your success.

Strikingly little has changed in human relations since Dale Carnegie wrote this guide to speaking in 1926, a decade before he gained international fame as the author of *How to Win Friends and Influence People*. When Carnegie produced this book he was making his living as the teacher of a popular seminar on public speaking. Carnegie had begun teaching his methods in 1912 at a YMCA in New York City. Requests for his course came in from around the country. By the mid-1930s, *Ripley's Believe-It-Or-Not* anointed Carnegie the king of public speaking with a cartoon reporting that he had personally critiqued 150,000 speeches.

Whether this is exaggerated, Carnegie's guidebook remains probably the best ever on how to speak with conviction and power. The book shows how to capture people's attention and win their confidence, whether you are speaking at a local club, a national sales conference, or in front of a class. But, as you will discover, this book delivers far more than instructions on how to give a good talk. Its greater value is that it teaches how to communicate effectively in virtually every sphere of life, on any occasion, and on behalf of any aim or purpose.

If you are a salesman, the book will help you will sell more. If you are a writer or editor, you will learn to better connect with readers. If you are an activist, you will find new ways to rally people to your cause.

What is the secret of Carnegie's formula? It comes down to three principles.

First, have an airtight knowledge of your subject—
know more than you need.

Second, when speaking, use plain language, personal examples, and tell stories of people.

Third, and finally, appeal to your listeners' sense of self-interest: We all crave safety, success, health, and prosperity. We also have a yearning for justice and fairness. Speak on these points, and you will likely bring people to your side.

Unless you are one of a very few naturally gifted speakers, implementing these simple guidelines requires persistence, inspiration, and strategy. You will find all of that—and more—in this book.

Carnegie's methods will bring you increased power. Use it for good ends.

—Mitch Horowitz

Chapter One

Developing Courage and Self-Confidence

Thousands of businessmen have taken my public-speaking courses. The vast majority have told me the same thing: "When I am called upon to stand up and speak, I become so self-conscious, so frightened, that I can't think clearly, can't concentrate, and can't remember what I wanted to say. I want to gain self-confidence, poise, and the ability to think on my feet."

Gaining self-confidence and courage, and the ability to think calmly and clearly while talking to a group, is not nearly as difficult as most imagine. It is not a gift bestowed by Providence. It is like the ability to play golf. Anyone can develop his own latent capacity, if he has sufficient desire to do so.

Rather than being frightened to speak publicly, you ought to think and speak *better* in front of a group. Their presence ought to lift and stir you. Many speakers will tell you that an audience is a stimulus, an inspiration that drives their brains to function more clearly, more keenly. At such times, thoughts, facts, and ideas that they did not know they possessed come to them. This will probably be your experience if you practice and persevere.

In order to get the most from this book, and to get it quickly, four things are essential:

FIRST

Start with a persistent desire. This is of far greater importance than you may realize. If I could look into your heart and mind right now, and ascertain the depth of your desires, I could foretell with near-certainty the swiftness of your progress. If your desire is pale and flabby, your achievements will be the same. But if you go after this subject with persistence, nothing will defeat you. Therefore, arouse your enthusiasm for this study. Think of what additional self-confidence and speaking ability will mean to you. Think of what it may mean in profits. Think of what it may mean socially—of the friends it will bring, of the increase of your personal influence, of the leadership it will give you.

SECOND

Know thoroughly what you intend to talk about. Unless a speaker has thought out and planned what he is going to say, he can't feel very comfortable when facing his auditors. An unprepared speaker *ought* to be self-conscious—and ought to be ashamed of his negligence.

THIRD

Act confident. "To feel brave," advises philosopher William James, "act as if we *were* brave, use all our will to that end, and a courage-fit will very likely replace the fit of fear." To develop courage when facing an audience, act as if you already have it. Unless you are prepared, of course, all the acting in the world will amount to little.

FOURTH

Practice! Practice! Practice! This is the most vital point of all. The first way, the last way, the never-failing way to overcome fear and develop self-confidence in speaking is—to speak. The whole matter finally simmers down to one essential: *practice*.

CHAPTER TWO

Self-Confidence Through Preparation

I t has been my professional duty, as well as my pleasure, to listen to and criticize approximately six thousand speeches a year. Most were made by ordinary businesspeople. If that experience has engraved one thing on my mind it is this: the urgent necessity of preparing a talk before one starts to make it, and of having something clear and definite to say.

Aren't you unconsciously drawn to a speaker who you feel has a real message, which he zealously desires to communicate? That is half the secret of speaking. When a speaker is in that kind of mental and emotional state he will discover a significant fact: his talk almost makes itself. A well-prepared speech is already nine-tenths delivered. The one fatal mistake is neglecting to prepare. "Perfect love," wrote the apostle John, "casteth out fear." So does perfect preparation.

What is preparation? Reading a book? That is one kind, but not the best. Reading may help; but if one attempts to lift a lot of "canned" thoughts out of a book and give them out as his own, the whole performance will be lacking.

Does preparation mean pulling together some faultless phrases, written down or memorized? No. Does it mean assembling a few casual thoughts that really convey very little to you personally? Not at all.

It means assembling *your* thoughts, *your* ideas, *your* convictions, *your* urges. You have them everyday of your life. They swarm through your dreams. Your whole existence has been filled with feelings and experiences. These things are lying deep in your subconscious as thick as pebbles on the seashore. Preparation means thinking, brooding, recalling, selecting the ones that speak to you most, polishing them, working them into a pattern, a mosaic of your own. That doesn't sound so difficult, does it? It isn't. It just requires a little concentration and thinking to a purpose.

What topics should you speak on? Anything that truly interests you. Ask yourself all possible questions concerning your topic. For example, if you are to speak on divorce, ask yourself what causes divorce, what are the effects economically, socially, domestically? Should we have uniform divorce laws? Should divorce be more difficult? Easier?

When preparing a speech, assemble a hundred thoughts, and discard ninety. Collect more material than there is any possibility of using. Get it for that additional confidence it will give you, for that sureness of touch. Get it for the effect it will have on your mind and heart and whole manner of speaking. That is a basic factor of preparation—yet most speakers constantly ignore it.

You must practice your speaking. If you stand up and think clearly and keep going for two or three minutes, that is a perfect way to practice delivering a talk. Try this a few times. What you can do first on a small scale you can do later on a large scale.

When making your practice talk, do not attempt to tell us everything in three minutes. It can't be done. Take one, and only one, phase of your topic: expand and enlarge that. For example, you can tell us how you came to be in your particular business or profession. Was it due to accident or choice? Relate your early struggles, your defeats, your hopes, and your triumphs. Give us a human-interest narrative, a real-life picture based on first-hand experience. The truthful, inside story of almost anyone's life—if told modestly and without egotism—is sure-fire speech material.

Many wonder if they should use notes while speaking. As a listener, don't notes destroy about fifty percent of your interest in a talk? Notes prevent, or at least render difficult, a very precious intimacy that ought to exist between the speaker and the audience. They create an air of artificiality. They restrain an audience from feeling that a speaker has confidence, spontaneity, and power.

Make notes during your preparation—elaborate ones, profuse ones. You may wish to refer to them when you are practicing your talk alone. You may possibly feel more comfortable if you have them stored away in your pocket when facing an audience. But they should be emergency tools, used only in case of a total wreck.

If you *must* use notes while speaking, make them extremely brief and write them in large letters on an ample sheet of paper. Then arrive early where you are speaking and discretely place your notes on the lectern, or conceal them behind books on a table. Glance at them if you must, but be brief.

In a few limited instances it may be wise to use notes. Some people during their first few talks are so nervous that they are unable to remember what they wanted to say. In such cases, it is fine to hold a few very condensed notes in your hands.

Get comfortable with your talk. After you have thought it out and arranged it, practice it silently as you walk along the street. Also get off somewhere by yourself and go over it from beginning to end, using gestures, letting yourself go. Imagine that you are addressing a real audience. The more of this you do, the more comfortable you will feel when the time comes to deliver your talk.

CHAPTER THREE

Keeping Your Audience Awake

What is the secret of success? "Nothing great," said Ralph Waldo Emerson, "was ever achieved without enthusiasm." This quality is the most effective, most important factor in advertising, selling goods, and getting things done.

I once put considerable reliance on the *rules* of public speaking. But with the passing of years I have come to put more and more faith in the *spirit* of speaking.

Remember always that every time we speak we determine the attitude of our listeners. If we are lackadaisical, they will be lackadaisical. If we are reserved, they will be reserved. If we are only mildly concerned, they will be only mildly concerned. But if we are deadly in earnest about what we say, and if we say it with feeling and spontaneity and force and conviction, they cannot keep from catching our spirit to a degree.

So, to feel earnest and enthusiastic, stand up and *act* in earnest and *be* enthusiastic. Stop leaning against the table. Stand tall. Stand still. Don't rock back and forth. Don't bob up and down. Don't shift your weight from one foot to the other and back again. In short, don't make a lot of nervous movements. They proclaim your lack of ease and self-possession. Control yourself physically. It conveys a sense of poise and power. Fill your lungs with oxygen. Look straight at your audience. Look at them as if you have something urgent to say. Look at them with the confidence and courage of a teacher, for you *are* a teacher, and they are there to hear you and to be taught.

Use emphatic gestures. Never mind, just now, whether they are beautiful or graceful. Think only of making them forceful and spontaneous. Make them now, not for the sense they will convey to others, but for what they will do for *you*. And they will do wonders. Even if you are speaking to a radio audience, *gesture, gesture*. Your gestures won't, of course, be visible to the hearers, but the result of your gestures will be audible to them. They will give increased aliveness and energy to your tone.

I have made a special study of Abraham Lincoln as a public speaker. He is perhaps the most loved man

America has ever produced; and unquestionably he delivered some of America's greatest speeches. Although he was a genius in some ways, I am inclined to believe that his power with audiences was due, in large measure, to his sympathy and honesty and goodness. He loved people. "His heart," said his wife, "is as large as his arms are long." He was Christlike.

The finest thing in speaking is neither physical nor mental. It is spiritual. Jesus loved men and their hearts burned within them as He talked with them by the way. If you want a splendid text on public speaking, read your New Testament.

CHAPTER FOUR

The Secret of Good Delivery

We are often told to be natural, to be ourselves. But the same society that gives this advice often bleeds naturalness out of us by imposing all kinds of preconceptions of just what "naturalness" ought to be.

The problem of teaching or training people in delivery is not one of superimposing additional characteristics; it is largely one of removing impediments, of freeing people, of getting them to speak, albeit with a different vocabulary and judgment, as they did when they were four years old.

As you practice, if you find yourself talking in a stilted manner, pause and say sharply to yourself mentally: "What is wrong? Wake up. Be human." In the end, even the matter of delivery comes back to a point that has already been emphasized: namely, *put your heart in your talks.*

Here are four things that all of us do unconsciously and naturally in conversation. You should do them when speaking in public.

1. Stress the important words in a sentence and subordinate the unimportant ones. When you speak conversationally you naturally give emphasis to keywords, such as *ambition, affliction,* and *skyscraper.* But not to unimportant words, such as *the, and,* or *but.*

2. Allow the pitch of your voice to flow up and down the scale from high to low and back again—as the pitch of a little child does when speaking.

3. Vary your rate of speaking, running rapidly over the unimportant words, spending more time on the ones you wish to make stand out.

4. And, finally, pause before and after your important ideas.

This is exactly how you speak to your friends, coworkers, or spouse—and it is how you should address an audience.

Chapter Five

Platform Presence and Personality

Personality—with the exception of *preparation* and *ideas*—is probably the most important factor in public speaking. But personality is a vague and elusive thing. It is the whole combination of the man: the physical, the spiritual, the mental; his traits, his predilections, his tendencies, his temperament, his cast of mind, his vigor, his experience, his training, his life.

If you wish to make the most of your individuality, go before your audience well rested. A tired person is not magnetic or attractive. When you have to make an important talk, beware of your hunger. Eat as sparingly as a saint. Do nothing to dull your senses or energy.

To maintain high spirits in the room, make sure that your audience—whether it is large or small—is grouped closely together. No audience will be easily moved when it is scattered. Nothing so dampens enthusiasm as wide, open spaces and empty chairs between the listeners.

If you are going to talk to a small group, choose a small room. Better to pack the aisles of a small place than to have people dispersed through the lonely, deadening spaces of a large hall. If your hearers are scattered, ask them to move down front and be seated near you. Insist on this before you start speaking.

Unless the audience is a fairly large one, and there is a real reason, a necessity, for you to stand on a platform, do not do so. Get down on the same level with your listeners. Stand near them. Break up all formality. Get an intimate contact. Make the thing conversational.

Take a deep breath. Look over your audience for a moment. If there is a noise or disturbance, pause until it quiets down. Hold your chest high. But why wait until you get before an audience to do this? Do it daily in private life. Then you will do it unconsciously in public.

And what shall you do with your hands? Forget them. If they fall naturally to your sides, that is ideal. And this returns us to the much-abused question of gesture. A man's gestures, like his toothbrush, should be very personal things. As all of us are different, our gestures will be individual if only we act natural. No two people should be drilled to gesture in precisely the same fashion.

I can't give you rules for gesturing—and neither can anyone else. For everything depends on the temperament of the speaker, upon his preparation, his enthusiasm, his personality, the subject, the audience, the occasion. Above all, be truthful; be comfortable; be yourself.

CHAPTER SIX

How to Open a Talk

For some unfortunate reason, the novice often feels that he ought to be funny as a speaker. So he is inclined to open with a humorous story, especially if the occasion is an after-dinner affair. The chances are his stories don't "click." In the immortal language of Hamlet, they prove "weary, stale, flat, and unprofitable."

In the difficult realm of speechmaking, what is more difficult, more rare, than the ability to make an audience laugh? Remember, it is seldom the story that is funny. It is *the way it is told* that makes it a success. Ninety-nine people out of a hundred will fail woefully with the identical stories that made Mark Twain famous.

The second egregious blunder that the beginner is likely to make in his opening is this: He apologizes. "I am no speaker . . . I am not prepared to talk . . . I have nothing to say . . ." Don't! Don't! Why insult your audience by suggesting that you did not think them worth preparing for, that just any old thing you happened to have on the fire would be good enough to serve them? We don't want to hear your apologies. We are there to be informed and interested—to be *interested,* remember that.

Arouse your audience's curiosity with your first sentence—and you have their attention. An article in *The Saturday Evening Post* entitled "With the Gangsters," began: "Are gangsters really organized? As a rule they are. How?" With ten words the writer announced his subject, told you something about it, and aroused your curiosity.

Everyone who aspires to speak in public ought to study the techniques that magazine writers use to immediately hook the reader's interest. You can learn far more from them about how to open a speech than you can by studying collections of speeches.

Chapter Seven

How to Close a Talk

I f you want to know how to end a speech, you can do no better than study the close of Lincoln's Second Inaugural:

With malice toward none, with charity for all, with firmness in the right as God gives us to see the right, let us strive on to finish the work we are in, to bind up the nation's wounds, to care for him who shall have borne the battle and for his widow and his orphan, to do all which may achieve and cherish a just and lasting peace among ourselves and with all nations.

You have just encountered what is, in my opinion, the most beautiful speech ending ever delivered. But you are not going to deliver immortal pronouncements as president in Washington or prime minister in Ottawa.

Your problem, perhaps, will be how to close a simple talk before a group of businessmen. How shall you set about it? Here are some suggestions.

FIRST

Even in a short talk of three to five minutes, a speaker is very apt to cover so much ground that at the close his listeners are a little hazy about all his main points. Some anonymous Irish politician is reported to have given this famous recipe for making a speech: "First, tell them what you are going to tell them; then, tell them; then, tell them what you told them." It is often highly advisable to "tell them what you told them." Briefly, of course, speedily—a mere outline, a summary.

SECOND

Try closing with a poetical quotation. If you can get a proper verse of poetry for your closing, it is almost ideal. It will give the desired flavor. It will give dignity. It will give individuality. It will give beauty. A choice Biblical quotation often has a profound effect.

THIRD

Build to a climax. The climax is a popular way of ending. It is often difficult to manage and is not an ending for all speakers or all subjects. But, when well done, it is excellent. It works up to a crest, a peak, getting stronger sentence by sentence. It often means ending with a tribute to someone or something, or an appeal for action—a topic we will cover in a future chapter.

CHAPTER EIGHT

How to Make
Your Meaning Clear

Napoleon's most emphatic instruction to his secretaries was: "Be clear! Be clear!"

When the disciples asked Christ why He taught the public by parables, He answered: "Because they seeing, see not; and hearing, hear not; neither do they understand."

And when you talk about a subject strange to your hearers, can you hope that they will understand you any more readily than people understood the Master?

Hardly. So what can we do about it? What did he do? He solved it in the most simple and natural manner imaginable: described the things people did not know by likening them to things they did know. The kingdom of Heaven . . . what would it be like?

"The kingdom of Heaven is like unto leaven . . . The kingdom of Heaven is like unto a merchant seeking goodly pearls . . . The kingdom of Heaven is like unto a net that was cast into the sea."

That was lucid; they could understand that. The housewives in the audience were using leaven every week; the fishermen were casting their nets into the sea daily; the merchants were dealing in pearls.

I once heard a lecturer on Alaska who failed, in many places, to be either clear or interesting because he neglected to talk in terms of what his audience knew. He told us, for example, that Alaska had a gross area of 590,804 miles.

Half-a-million square miles—what does that mean to the average person? Precious little. He is not used to thinking in square miles. They conjure up no mental picture. He does not have any idea whether half-a-million square miles are approximately the size of Maine or Texas. Suppose the speaker had said that the coastline of Alaska and its islands is longer than the distance around the globe, and that its area more than equals the combined areas of Vermont, New Hampshire, Maine, Massachusetts, Rhode Island, Connecticut, New York, New Jersey, Pennsylvania, Delaware, Maryland, West Virginia, North Carolina, South Carolina, Georgia, Florida, Mississippi, and Tennessee. Would that not give everyone a fairly clear conception of the area of Alaska?

If you belong to a profession that does technical work—if you are a lawyer, physician, engineer, or are in a highly specialized line of businesses—be doubly careful when you talk to outsiders to express yourself in *plain terms*, and to fill in necessary details.

Put your ideas into language plain enough for any boy to understand.

Chapter Nine

How to Interest
Your Audience

What would you say are the three most interesting subjects in the world? They are: *sex, property,* and *religion*. By the first we can create life, by the second we maintain it, and by the third we hope to continue it in the world to come.

But it is *our* sex, *our* property, and *our* religion that interests us. Our interests swarm around our own egos.

When a British newspaper baron was asked what interests people, he answered with one word: "themselves." Do you want to know what kind of person you are? Ah, now we are on an interesting topic. We are talking about *you*.

Remember that people spend most of their time, when they are not concerned with the problems of business, thinking about and justifying and glorifying themselves. The average man will be more wrought up over a dull razor than over a revolution in South America. His own toothache will distress him more than an earthquake in Asia destroying half-a-million lives. He would rather listen to you say some nice thing about him than hear you discuss the ten greatest men in history.

A successful magazine editor once told me the secret of capturing people's attention: "People are selfish," he said. "They are interested chiefly in themselves. They are not very much concerned about whether the government should own the railroads; but they do want to know how to get ahead, how to draw more salary, how to keep healthy, how to take care of their teeth, how to take baths, how to keep cool in the summer, how to get a job, how to handle employees, how to buy homes, how to remember, how to avoid grammatical errors, and so one. People are always interested in human stories, so I have some rich man tell how he made a million in real estate. I get prominent bankers and presidents of various corporations to tell their stories of how they battled their way up to power and wealth."

This editor has attracted millions of readers by appealing to their selfish interests.

But interest is also *contagious*. Your hearers are almost sure to catch it if you have a bad case of it yourself. A short time ago I heard a speaker warn his audience that if the present methods of catching rockfish in Chesapeake Bay were continued the species would become extinct. And in a very few years! He *felt* his subject. It was important. He was in real earnest about it. When he finished all of us probably would have been willing to sign a petition to protect the rockfish by law.

Always remember, your audience will feel interested in your topic to the degree that you are sincerely interested in it yourself.

CHAPTER TEN

Improving Your Language

The world judges us by four things: by what we do, by how we look, by what we say, and by how we say it.

Many people blunder through life with no conscious effort to enrich their stock of words, to master their shades of meaning, and to speak with precision. Many people habitually use the overworked and exhausted phrases of the office and street. Small wonder that their way of speaking lacks distinction and individuality.

But how are we to become intimate with words, to speak them with beauty and accuracy? Fortunately, there is no mystery about the means to be employed. *Books!* There is the secret. He who would enlarge his stock of words must drink deeply of good literature.

Lincoln wrote to a young man eager to become a successful lawyer: "It is only to get the books, and read and study them carefully . . . Work, work, work is the main thing."

What books? Begin with Arnold Bennett's *How to Live on Twenty-Four Hours a Day*. This book is as stimulating as a cold bath. It tells you a lot about that most interesting of all subjects—yourself. It reveals how much time you are wasting each day, how to stop the wastage, and how to use what you salvage.

To learn about greatness, make Ralph Waldo Emerson your daily companion. Command him first to give you his famous essay on "Self-Reliance." Read it again and again. Dedicate yourself to Emerson's essays and you will encounter some of the highest thoughts and finest uses of words in the English language.

Finally, don't use shopworn, threadbare words and expressions. Be exact in your meaning. Avoid trite comparisons such as "cool as a cucumber" or "high as a kite." Strive for freshness. Create expressions of your own. Have the courage to be distinctive.

CHAPTER ELEVEN

How to Get Action

If you could have the power of any talent that you now possess doubled and tripled, which one would you select? Wouldn't you likely designate your ability to influence others, to get action? That would mean additional power, additional profit, and additional pleasure.

Must this art—so essential to our success in life—remain forever a hit-and-miss affair? Must we blunder along depending upon our instinct, upon rule-of-thumb methods only? Or is there a more intelligent way to achieve it?

There is, and we shall discuss it at once—a method based on the rules of common sense, on the rules of human nature, a method that I have frequently, and successfully, used myself.

The first step in this method is to gain *interested attention*. Unless you do that people will not listen closely to what you say. We've already touched on some of the ways to do this: Talk to people about topics of vital interest—usually themselves. Be deeply in earnest about what you say. Be clear, plainspoken, and definite as to what you mean.

The second step is to gain the *confidence* of your hearers. Unless you do that, they will have no faith in what you say. And here is where many speakers fall down. Here is where many advertisements fail, where many business letters, many employees, many business enterprises go nowhere. Here is where many individuals fail to make themselves effective within the human environment.

The prime way to win confidence is to *deserve it.* I have noticed time without number that facile and witty speakers—if those are their chief qualities—are not nearly as effective as those who are less brilliant but more sincere. There is no use trying to pretend a sympathy or sincerity that one does not feel. It won't work. It must be genuine.

The second way to gain the confidence of the audience is to speak discretely out of your own experience. This helps immensely. If you give opinions, people may question them. If you relate hearsay or repeat what you have read, it may have a second-hand flavor. But what *you yourself have lived through*, that has a genuine ring of truth and veracity. And people like it. They believe it.

Once you have won people's confidence, consider what people are looking for—from you and from the world around them. One of the strongest of human motives is *the desire for gain*. And even stronger than the money motive is the desire for *self-protection*. All health appeals are based on that. To make an appeal to someone's sense of self-protection, make it personal. Don't, for example, quote statistics to show that cancer is on the rise. No. Tie it right down to the people who are listening to you, for example: "There are thirty people in this room. If all of you live to be forty-five, three of you, according to the law of medical averages, will die of cancer."

As strong as the desire for money—and for many even stronger—is the wish to be well regarded, to be admired. In other words, pride. Ask yourself why you bought this book. Were you influenced, to some extent, by the wish to make a better impression? Did you covet the flow of inward satisfaction that comes from making a commendable talk? Won't you feel a very pardonable pride in the power, leadership, and distinction that naturally flow to the good public speaker?

There is another powerful group of motives that influence us mightily. We shall call them religious motives. I mean religious not in the sense of orthodox worship or the tenets of any particular creed or sect. I mean rather that broad group of beautiful and eternal truths that Christ taught: justice and forgiveness and mercy, serving others and loving our neighbors as ourselves.

No man likes to admit, even to himself, that he is not good and kind and magnanimous. So we love to be appealed to on these grounds. It implies a certain nobleness of soul. We take pride in that.

To summarize all we have been discussing, here are the ways that you as a speaker can get people on your side and move them to action:

FIRST
Get interested attention.

SECOND
Win confidence by deserving it, not only by your sincerity but also by being qualified to speak on your subject, by telling us the things that experience has taught you.

THIRD
State your facts clearly and educate your audience regarding the merits of your proposal or cause.

FOURTH
Appeal to the motives that make us act: the desire for gain, self-protection, pride, pleasures, sentiments, affec-

tions, and religious ideals, such as justice, mercy, forgiveness, and love.

These methods, if used wisely, will not only help the speaker in public, but also in private. They will help him in the writing of sales letters, in constructing advertisements, in managing business interviews—and in making an impact in life.

Born in northwestern Missouri in 1888, DALE CARN-EGIE was one of the pioneers of motivational and self-help philosophy. World famous for his 1936 classic, *How to Win Friends and Influence People*, Carnegie began his career as a writer and teacher in 1912 when he offered courses on public speaking at a YMCA in New York City. Carnegie was one of the first business minds of the twentieth century to grasp the importance of being able to communicate ideas and concepts clearly to colleagues, coworkers, clients, and customers. His pioneering book, *Public Speaking: A Practical Course for Business Men*, from which this volume is abridged, first appeared in 1926. It is regarded as the seminal work on how to speak with power and skill. Carnegie died in New York City in 1955.

MITCH HOROWITZ, who abridged and introduced this volume, is the PEN Award-winning author of books including *Occult America* and *The Miracle Club: How Thoughts Become Reality*. *The Washington Post* says Mitch "treats esoteric ideas and movements with an even-handed intellectual studiousness that is too often lost in today's raised-voice discussions." Follow him @MitchHorowitz.

HOW TO
ATTRACT
GOOD LUCK

HOW TO
ATTRACT
GOOD LUCK

by A.H.Z. Carr

The Unparalleled Classic On Lucky Living

Abridged and Introduced
by Mitch Horowitz

THE CONDENSED CLASSICS LIBRARY™

Contents

Contents

Good Luck Is No Accident

D o you want good luck? Of course you do. We all depend, to one degree or another, on fortuitous opportunities to put our skills to use, to meet people who provide vital openings for us, and to discover information that makes a crucial difference in our lives.

You are about to experience a condensation of one of the most intriguing and little-known books in the self-help tradition: *How to Attract Good Luck*. The book offers a straightforward and ethical recipe for cultivating your ability to identify and prepare for those crucial moments where life's currents lift you, or at least help you along. The title *How to Attract Good Luck* may sound like it belongs to a gambling guide. But this book is the furthest thing from it.

Economist, journalist, and diplomat A.H.Z. Carr wrote *How to Attract Good Luck* in 1952. Carr had

served as an economic adviser in the presidential administrations of Franklin Roosevelt and Harry Truman,
and spent time on economic and diplomatic missions
in Europe and the Far East. He amassed a great deal
of experience observing how most personal misfortune
arises from impetuous, shortsighted, or unethical behavior. By "luck" Carr was referring not to blind chance
but rather to how we can bend circumstances to our
favor through specific patterns of behavior.

In an entertaining and incisive fashion, his book
catalogues the insights he gleaned on how *virtue pays*.
In a certain sense, Carr's book is really a guide to hon-
orable living, which, in his estimation, pays dividends
in success, stability, and peace of mind. Carr's work is
an exegesis of a statement attributed to scientist Louis
Pasteur: "Chance favors the prepared mind." Preparation, in Carr's view, is based not only in rigor and study,
but also in a kind of personal comportment that makes
one ready to take authority or act decisively when the
need arises.

In an age where people gobble up copies of bla-
tantly amoral success guides like *The 48 Laws to Power*,
I find something distinctly appealing and rock-solid in
Carr's work. This is a self-help book that can be used
by someone who tries to live by the Beatitudes or the
Boy Scouts Code of Honor. And why *wouldn't* we want

to live by enduring guides to decency and ethic solidity? Carr tells us, in effect, that we can both achieve in the world and remain appealing as people. In fact, he maintains, very persuasively, that sound behavior and achievement are intimately united. Do you doubt that? Put his ideas to the test.

Without sardonicism or irony, I wish you a heartfelt *good luck*.

—Mitch Horowitz

CHAPTER ONE

Chance Versus Luck

People have always sought ways to improve their luck. Their efforts have generally centered around portents, omens, and black magic. The Roman augur, interpreting the flights of birds, has been succeeded in modern times by numerologists and clairvoyants. But these practices have degraded the subject of luck. At the very mention of the word, many intelligent people understandably lift a skeptical eyebrow.

But our understanding of luck can be lifted from a black-cat level to an infinitely higher and broader plane. Psychology has opened the gate to a new and rational approach to luck. Armed with modern insights, those who seek can discover the true nature of luckiness. Luck is not a mere matter of poker winnings and the like but rather a *specific condition of mind*. This book shows how the lucky condition of mind can be attained.

At the outset, we must clarify the difference between "chance" and "luck." Chance comprises the infinite number of unpredictable happenings, both great and trivial, that are constantly at work in the world, whether a volcanic eruption or a sparrow's flight. Most of the chances we perceive in life seem remote and meaningless. But now and then a chance will touch the interests of an individual—and then it becomes very personal and significant indeed. *For as soon as human emotions are affected by a chance, it has been transformed into luck.* Luck, then, is the effect of chance on our lives.

But—and this is of vital importance—chance is not the only element in luck. Another factor is involved—ourselves. For it is our *response* to chance that provides the counterpoint in the harmony of events that we call luck. Whether and how a chance affects us is largely determined by our own attitude and behavior. Chance and response, between them, provide the warp and woof of existence, and the pattern of every life.

The central theme of this book is: *We can improve our luck by making ourselves readier for the chances of life as they come to us.* Shakespeare put it this way: "If it be not now, yet it will come. The readiness is all." These words have profound meaning. For the vigor of effort that we make to be ready for luck may well be the deciding factor between a lucky and unlucky life.

It lies within our power to influence, not chance, but our relation to chance. And in that sense none of us can escape a measure of responsibility for his own luck.

Chapter Two

How Zest Exposes Us to Luck

Good luck usually strikes into the world of men with the suddenness of lightening. How can we attract this beneficent lightening in our lives?

Over many years hundreds of people have told me their stories of good luck. More than half of them had one thing in common: the lucky episode began for the person concerned at a time when he was exposed to others—*when someone else unexpectedly said something important to him.* Most of our good luck—the beneficial effect of chance upon our lives—comes to us through other people. To expose ourselves to luck, then, means in essence to come into healthy human relationships with more people. The more luck-lines a person throws out, the more luck he is likely to find.

A high proportion of lucky chances comes to us through strangers, or people we know only slightly.

This is not really surprising. Most of our well-worn con-
tacts rarely offer us a new perspective, or a new piece
of important information. But displaying "unexpected
friendlessness" toward people we do not know is the secret of much of the luck of life. Ancient myths and parables repeatedly tell of rewards heaped upon someone
who is kind to a travelling stranger—only to discover
that the seeming stranger is a god or angel.

Of course, not every stranger merits our trust. We
must guard against the aggressive bore, the gossip, or
the ruthless peddler. But do not allow fear or indif-
ference to block you off to the potential luck of The
Stranger.

In enabling us to throw out luck-lines to strangers and old acquaintances alike, one quality has almost
magical power—the quality of zest. Philosopher Ber-
trand Russell has called zest "the most universal and
distinctive mark of happy men." Zest is also the mark
of most lucky men—a quality which, in the struggle of
life, often overshadows and outweighs serious character
flaws and limitations of mind.

Never confuse zest with greed or gluttony. Zest
means to take an explorer's interest in the world. The
zestful person upon meeting others is curious not what
they may think of him, how much money they make, or
what they can do for him. Rather, he wants to discover

their personalities and ways of life. He is capable of sincere enthusiasm, praise, and appreciation. The zestful person may feel angered or disquieted by events, but he loves life in all its follies. We need zest to counteract feelings of anxiety, which lay waste to human relationships.

Experimentation of almost any kind leads to zest. So does the discovery of a meaningful avocation or hobby—any well-defined core activity that stimulates thought and beckons new skill.

Frequently the things we read with zest are coupled directly with strokes of luck. Even a sentence or two, found by chance, can set off a train of lucky events. This is why books have a special place in luck development. The effort of attention needed to read a book, and especially a book with serious content, impresses it strongly on the memory, so that its ideas can be readily evoked by passing chance and brought into lucky use.

Chapter Three

How Generosity Invites Luck

Some people put out luck-lines that get them nowhere. Things may start out all right but they find that instead of good luck they have been tempting misfortune. Sometimes we reach out to people—but our *unchecked* ego gets in our way.

Probably no human frailty is more likely to bring bad luck than an exaggerated need for appreciation. This unhappy state of mind, which usually grows out of a rooted feeling of insecurity, drives its victim to advertise his importance and demand that the busy world pay attention to him. The egotist tends to be inattentive when others are talking, he causes acquaintances to take a passive position in conversation and to therefore withhold valuable information and ideas. Even more serious, such a person tends to brag and boast, if sometimes in subtle and indirect ways.

The chronic egotist is always a candidate for bad luck. But the strong characteristic opposite to egotism, generosity of spirit, consistently acts as a magnet for favorable chances.

Note that we're speaking of *uncalculated generosity*. A distinction should also be drawn between genuine generosity and the compulsive and almost frantic displays of giving which some neurotic people make.

The luck that comes to us as a result of true generosity seldom takes the form of spectacular, immediate blessings out the blue. The real reward of the generous is invisible and secret. It lies partly in their own psychological health and partly in the hearts of others—in the reservoir of good will they build up. The generous person creates an unsuspected potential of good luck that needs only a touch from chance to burst all at once into happy reality.

In luck-development we need to keep in mind this seemingly obvious yet easily neglected fact: *In order to have real friends, a man must be capable of being one.* We can, for example, try a little hard to understand the problems of a friend, and give him such assistance as we're able without seeking return. When a friend is suffering, we can suppress remarks that would only add to his pain. Likewise, when a friend is fortunate, we can fight down our envy and try to enter his gladness.

The key point is that *every act of true friendship and generosity is proof of a rising luck-potential within us.*

Chapter Four

Turning Points

It is actually possible to anticipate favorable chances. Chance, which produces the effects in our lives that we call luck, has its own way of behaving. We need to become aware of two marked tendencies in the fall of chance: *rhythm* and *interconnection*.

Chance follows the same rhythm of nature. It is not an even, unbroken rhythm. We can learn to expect the alternation of runs of chance; moreover we can learn to expect it more at certain times than others. *The runs of chance in life are normally short.* After similar chances have appeared in succession several times, we have every reason to expect a change. This calls for expectancy and alertness.

As the rhythm of chance often points to the turning points of life, so does the characteristic that I have called *interconnection*. From time to time, two or more interlocking chances in close succession touch almost every life. And it is at these points where luck reveals its power most dramatically. At such times, by alertness, we can often "pyramid" our luck, using the luck of the first chance as a steppingstone to the greater luck of the others.

It is a fact of many, and perhaps most lives, that large fulfillments come not at a steady pace but by sudden leaps. After a single lucky chance we are wise to keep all of our senses alert for other chances that may interlock with the first, and provide a major turning point of life. The conscious effort to be alert to chance seems especially productive of turning points in periods of pronounced social change, when the old order is upturned.

Enthusiasm for the spectacular and impatience with the commonplace chances of life are likely to result in peaks of good luck alternating with deep valleys of misfortune. The reservoir of luck in each of us is far more often tapped by chance in frequent little jets than in big bursts.

We must also keep alert in the face of *crucial chances*. To do so we need to maintain our physical energy at a high level. A sound regimen of diet, sleep, and exercise, helps assure the ability of our alertness and mental acuity. Beyond this, we can generate alertness through *imaginative anticipation*. Obviously we cannot anticipate all eventualities, but we can often decide in advance what we shall do if certain common chances befall us.

Finally, when the occurrence of a chance seems fairly probable, a single preparatory action can go far to maintain the essential alertness until the event takes place.

CHAPTER FIVE

Our Desires and Our Luck

There is no reason to believe that opportunity knocks only once; but whether it knocks once, twice, or ten times, only the self-knowing mind, the mind that knows what it wants and what it will risk, is likely to recognize the real nature of the chance and act accordingly. Often the claims of competing desires are so strong as to make a decision difficult. No matter how complex the problem presented by chance, a firm set of values for our various desires helps us to find the lucky answer.

By testing chances against our personal values we sometimes perceive luck where others would see none. By knowing what you really want in life, you may detect opportunities that others may not understand or value.

Here is a core principle of life: *The person who knows the relative importance, for himself, of conflicting*

*desires is best prepared to recognize the favorable chance
as it passes, and to transform it into luck.* It is not easy to
prioritize your desires, but it is absolutely vital if you
want to bring more luck into your life. Fortunately,
modern psychology has greatly clarified this problem.
It tells us that a person's desires are not fixed and rigid;
rather, they are malleable, ever-changing, and evolv-
ing in us from cradle to grave.

As adults we have ten basic, universal desires:

1. Love, both romantic and the affections of friends
   and family.
2. Procreation, with the urge to sex, marriage, and
   children.
3. Group status, or a firm place in the community or
   group.
4. Prestige, or recognition by others of our talents and
   distinctions.
5. Economic security and a satisfying standard of
   living.
6. Self-respect, or a sense of living up to meritorious
   standards of behavior.
7. Self-expression, or the use of one's abilities and talents.
8. Faith, or belief in a universal purpose or goal out-
   side ourselves.

9. Long life, specifically the prospect of long-term physical and mental vigor.
10. Good health and freedom from illness.

The evaluation of desires is a highly personal matter. Everyone has, in effect, a private blend of desires. Some want more love than others, some more prestige, some more economic security, and so on. This difference profoundly affects our ideas of what is lucky. We must also distinguish honestly between basic desires versus compulsions or obsessions. Unchecked desires can balloon into obsessions or addictions, which destroy our luck.

Chapter Six

Our Abilities and Our Luck

O ne of the major elements in appraising the luck-content of a chance can be expressed in the question: *Does it accord with my abilities?* Unless our estimate of our abilities is realistic, we can be tempted by chance into foolhardy and disastrous ventures.

Part of the basic formula for a lucky life is: *Make the most of what you are, and do not try to be more than you can be.* The man who tries to live beyond his capacities, physically, psychologically, or economically, invites misfortune.

The more that you know about the requirements and hazards of a given chance, the more likely you are to find good luck in it, and avoid bad luck—*if you have a realistic understanding of your own abilities and limitations.* Nothing is more promising of good luck than the chance that accords with desire and ability; nothing is more dangerous than chance that appeals to desire but is not backed up by requisite ability.

So long as your judgment is mature and sound, there is a role for *inner conviction* in assessing one's abilities. When internal conviction asserts itself with sufficient power, it can often bring luck in spite of the most adverse judgments.

In sum, only when a given chance conforms both to basic desire and to demonstrated or indicated ability does it give genuine promise of good luck.

Chapter Seven

Judgment as an Element in Luck

Judgment has been called the eye of the mind. When people demonstrate bad judgment it is usually due less to defects in thinking than to emotional factors that have clouded the mind's outlook.

An appalling amount of bad luck can be attributed to three emotional states: boredom, anxiety, and over-confidence. Use these principles to your benefit: 1) Beware of boredom. 2) Allow for anxiety. 3) Overcome overconfidence. These rules are important markers on the road to better luck.

When a person is bored he hungers for an event that will lead to a better life. He looks with favor upon anything that seems to promise a thrill. This makes him highly vulnerable to bad luck because he does not assess the risks of the chances that he takes. Boredom has pushed many people into tragic misfortune.

Similarly in forming our judgment of chances, we must allow for inevitable and natural anxiety. Anxiety can cause us to reject favorable chances, even when they come straight at us, by making us think that we that we see peril and risk where there is none. In order to be lucky, we are not required to give up anxiety (some of which is healthy); but we must make allowances for the appearance of anxiety, and bring our fears to the surface for appropriate judgment.

In some ways, the more important rule for protecting our judgment from unstable emotions is the need to "overcome overconfidence." A dangerous sense of overconfidence can result from: 1) a run of luck, 2) a lack of experience, and 3) a misunderstanding of motive.

We sometimes believe that we understand people's motives when we actually do not. Too many of us accept, at face value, the motives put forward by people with whom we must deal in chance situations. Not that we need to be cynical about the motives of other people. Cynicism is, in truth, only an inverted form of naiveté, twisting one's view of reality. At the same time, when we have no sound reason to believe in the other person's purity of motive, we do well to pause for reflection.

Chapter Eight

Safeguarding Luck with Self-Respect

It is always unlucky to forfeit self-respect. The test of self-respect is especially important when chance demands an instantaneous decision and allows no time for judgment to probe and consider.

It is not always easy to tell which course of action in a complex situation will best maintain self-respect. And, curiously enough, some people even shrug at the term self-respect, failing to realize the decisive role it plays in good luck. They think that enjoying life is the only measure of success. The stifling of conscience, however, means that *the psychic trouble within us seeks other outlets*, such as the warping of the personality through neurotic fear or vicious criticism.

At the same time, there can be no doubt that self-respecting behavior frequently results in strong new luck-lines, over which material benefits flow. For example, the courage displayed by an act of selfless honesty, such as owning up to a serious mistake and not letting others take the fall for it, often marks someone as accountable and deserving of trust with serious responsibilities.

It is never too late to reaffirm self-respect. Fortunately for us, the occasional violence we do to our self-respect *is* only occasional. A single self-respecting action, taken when the personality was in danger of becoming permanently enfeebled, can perform a miracle of regeneration.

At this point a warning should be posted. It is easy to confuse self-respect with pride—and pride is a positively unlucky trait. In contrast to self-respect, pride—whether over origin, beauty, position, achievement, or anything else—is fundamentally an expression of insecurity, with its roots in illusion. It is a sign that someone is trying to cover up a feeling of spiritual weakness by pointing to a superficial advantage or external superiority.

When we sharply separate self-respect from pride and vanity, it serves us best in the selection and rejection of chances.

CHAPTER NINE

The Intuitive Approach to Luck

Below the threshold of consciousness is a kind of secret reference library of unspoken knowledge and forgotten impressions. The unconscious mind at certain times will pull out the evidence that bears on a risk before you, delivering its verdict in the mysterious form of *intuition*.

Our intuitive judgments of others may sometimes arise from unconscious impressions of previous experiences with people of similar characteristics. The wife of a friend once cautioned her husband to avoid Jim, a new acquaintance at work. The friend later told me: "Jim was a good fellow, but I felt highly competitive toward him. He brought out the worst in me." The wife had demonstrated sound intuition. No one can afford to forget that while he is influencing other people, they are also influencing him, for better or worse. Getting involved with competitive people often brings bad luck.

Little mishaps in the home or office have many times been preludes to larger misfortunes. This is certainly not to say that we should seek for omens. But there is nothing superstitious about recognizing the implications of our unconscious actions. Sigmund Freud stressed this point, noting: "The Roman who . . . withdrew from an undertaking because he had stumbled on his threshold . . . was a better psychologist than we . . . For his stumbling could demonstrate to him the existence of a doubt . . . the force of which could weaken the power of his intention at the moment of its execution. For only by concentrating all psychic forces on the desired aim can one be assured of its success."

Never confuse intuition with a mere *wish* for something. Apparent intuitions that coincide with feverish wishes, and which involve high risks—such as the desire to romantically win over an uninterested or deeply flawed lover—should always be regarded with suspicion.

CHAPTER TEN

The Power of the Response

Some acts of chance, like a fatal accident, leave no room for response. The vast realm of luck, however, is ruled not by chance alone but jointly, by chance and by ourselves.

Even seeming disasters can be converted or redirected by a sound response, which makes us more educated, more resilient, and more knowledgeable. Sometimes the response may aid us in some other area that seems distant from the event itself.

Underlying the sound responses of lucky people to chance are three predominant character traits: *high energy, vigorous imagination, and strong faith.*

These are the "big three" that can transform raw chance into good fortune. If you are lacking in one or two of these and are willing to try to do something about it, that willingness alone is the gateway to better luck. A vigorous effort to develop ourselves in any lucky direction can itself bring us into closer harmony with chance.

We will now review the importance of each trait, and how to strengthen it.

Chapter Eleven

How Increased Energy Produces Luck

Here is a statement so obvious that one may easily lose sight of its significance: *Much of our greatest luck comes to us when our energy is high.* Heightened energy manifests itself to us in a number of specifically luck ways—sometimes in a display of muscular power to meet a sudden chance, but more frequently in a state of mind. Notably, three psychology attitudes are closely linked to luck: *presence of mind, confidence, and determination.*

Presence of mind is a kind of alertness. As soon as we have identified the chance, the alert condition undergoes a profound change. We no longer watch concentratedly for something to happen. It has happened. Our problem now is how to respond. Instead of keeping attention focused entirely on the chance event, we survey our surroundings—we "get the picture"—we see what things or circumstances near us can be of use in responding to the chance. The more "present" our mind is, the more likely we are to respond luckily to the chance.

Confidence is vital to our luck development. Preparation induces confidence. Especially in those instances that involve other people, like your subject if you are a journalist, or your partners if you are an investor. *Preparatory study of the facts makes for luck.* Of course, no one is confident all the time, or in the face of all chances. Our need is to *use periods of high energy to prepare for the chances of life that seem most probable.*

Like confidence and presence of mind, the quality of **determination** is also associated with high energy. Some people are more determined than others because they are able to *renew their energy* in relation to an activity. Often a person has high energy at the outset of a project, but it dissipates. *Determination grows out of the repeated tapping of your energy reserves in the pursuit of a single purpose.* This usually occurs: 1) When you are focused on a definite purpose, and you keep your aim constantly in sight, stimulating hope and renewing incentive. 2) When you prevent yourself from growing stale through an occasional change of activity, which makes possible a zestful return to the attack.

High energy is in large degree the expression of an attitude toward life. "A single successful effort of moral volition," wrote William James, "such as saying 'no' to some habitual temptation, or performing some courageous act, will launch a man on a higher level of energy for days or weeks, will give him a new range of power."

It must also be said that anyone who fails to make an effort to eat and drink wisely, to get enough exercise and rest, and to shake off his worries, greatly weakens his power to respond successfully to life's chances. Any effort we make to raise the level of our energy by improvement in these essential aspects of living automatically tends to improve our luck potential.

Chapter Twelve

Imagination and Luck

Wherever luck is most impressive, it is usually because energy has been directed by imagination, which reveals the potentialities of a chance.

Not every imagination, as we all know, makes for good luck. Notably, the egocentric imagination, which evokes images concerned primarily with selfish gratifications, invites unluckiness. One of its distinguishing products is the *daydream*—the fantasy that is always concerned with the future of the dream and which leads to the fictional fulfillment of some desire. Heedlessly indulged, the daydream can be a menace to good luck. It weakens one's hold on reality and reduces the energy available for the real tasks of life.

Another unlucky way the egocentric imagination expresses itself is morbidity. The morbid imagination tends to focus on the unpleasant perceptions that fit into its dark and distorted picture of life, and to ignore constructive or encouraging elements. Where this condition exists, a trivial chance can easily produce a major increase of unhappiness.

The unmistakable characteristic of the healthy and lucky imagination is that it readily turns outward, away from the self. It does not confuse the world of external reality with the images conjured up by desire or anxiety. The healthy imagination also has a high capacity for empathy, which enables you to share in the feelings of others in given situations. A great part of human luck depends on other people. When we share in their states of mind, we are more likely to respond to chances in ways that link them to us emotionally, making for a greater probability of luck for all concerned.

Just as a strong empathic imagination can bring good luck out of unfavorable circumstances, such as forming a bond with a gifted person who has experienced a temporary setback, a counter weakness area can lead to disastrous failures. This is *irrational prejudice.* Irrational prejudice includes snobbishness, religious or racial bigotry, and class discrimination. The creeping vine of intolerance chokes off the empathic imagination. What's more, prejudice dwells in insecure minds, which are natural targets for trouble.

CHAPTER THIRTEEN

The Luckiness of Faith

The word "faith" is used here, not in the sense of conventional lip service to a religious creed, but to signify the state of mind of those who are either wholly at one with their religion, or who profoundly hold a philosophic belief from which flows an affirmation of life and a moral principle.

Sometimes men and women who have neither religion nor philosophy try to fill this void in their lives by pinning their faith on their children or their work. Love of one's children and respect for one's work can be strengthening influences. They cannot, however, take the psychological place of a profound identification between the self and some large religious or philosophic conviction of good, which provides a moral basis for behavior.

When we lack the steadying power of faith, the insecurity feelings latent in all of us tend to run away with our behavior. A psychologist recently made an informal study among his university students of three negative traits: bragging, snobbishness, and secretiveness, all of which express insecurity. When he correlated the results with what he knew of the students' backgrounds and beliefs, there seemed to be an unmistakable link between the presence of these unlucky flaws and the absence of religious or philosophic faith.

We can cite very specific reasons why luck is most likely to be found in the faith-directed way of life. Faith tends to develop in the individual certain attributes that go far to ensure successful responses to chance. Courage is one of these attributes. But no less important are two traits that are in good part the psychological offspring of faith: *integrity* and *sense of proportion*.

It is through integrity that faith chiefly affects our responses to chance. Not that we find integrity in every person who professes a religion or a philosophy. But whenever we do find a person of genuine integrity, there, almost by definition, we find a core of faith. The exaltation of moral principle manifests a belief in universal law.

Together with courage and integrity, a third lucky characteristic flows from faith—the wide-horizoned attitude of mind that we think of as a *sense of proportion*. This attitude expresses itself in the personality through humility and through humor. The man who sees his actual position in the universe, and who can endure the revelation of his personal unimportance, gains enormous inner strength. Throughout life the sense of proportion links with chance to produce good luck and to mitigate misfortune.

The same quality, the sense of proportion derived from religion or philosophy, has a further bearing on our fortunes through its power in combatting envy, among the unluckiest of human characteristics. Competitive beings that we are, we all experience envy. But if envy is quickly controlled by a sense of proportion, it does little harm. In fact, a feeling of envy may be transformed to admiration and spur you to make more of your abilities. The great polar explorer Amundsen said that when he heard that Commodore Peary had reached the North Pole, his first thought was, "Then I shall visit both Poles." And he did. The danger to luck arises when envy in unchecked and becomes a permanent state of mind, which engenders bitterness, scheming, and cynicism.

The envy-resisting sense of proportion, rooted integrity, and sustained courage—those are stars of luck's constellation; and faith is their parent-quality. The need of effort to develop these attributes is too plain to need much discussion. What must be stressed is the point that any such effort, if it is to succeed, must follow the spiritual and intellectual route toward faith.

Chapter Fourteen

The Will to Be Lucky

The conscious steering of our actions, which is the peculiar privilege of man, is a skill that must be learned. The successful steersman in life, the lucky man, requires a degree of mastery of difficult arts of behavior and self-expression. Certain specific qualities of character and personality must be developed in us before we can find a lucky way through life.

When men have a keen sense of responsibility for their own fortunes, they can influence their luck far more than they dream. The chances of life, from which luck flows, are a kind of cosmic committee, constantly testing our readiness for membership in the lodge of the lucky. The *will to be lucky* is the crux of our internal development.

To modify destructive habits, which often have strong roots, *we must feel active resentment of the insecurity feelings that push us into inferior patterns of behavior*—and that make us unlucky in life. That gives us the requisite strength of feeling to challenge and change depleting habits of behavior.

Any effort we make, however slight, to prevent the dictation of our behavior by insecurity feelings is a step toward luckiness. A single modest improvement at a time is often enough to produce far-reaching consequences in one's fortunes. We have examined the importance to our luck of a number of characteristics which have a close relationship to the workings of chance: zest and generosity, with the power to attract luck into our lives; alertness, self-knowledge, judgment, self-respect, and intuition—all of high value in the recognition of favorable chances; and qualities of special significance in our responses to chance—energy, with its bearing on the presence of mind, confidence, and determination—imagination—and courage, sense of proportion, and integrity, which grow out of faith.

By doing a few relatively simple things over a period of a few months, you can often develop the lucky side of your personality to an extent that can seem miraculous. Vast and ungovernable is the power of chance; and yet, as we have seen, its influence on our luck is profoundly shaped by our own actions. The presence of this book is itself a chance, and your response to it may go far to affect your fortune to come.

Chapter Fifteen

Lucky Habits: Takeaway Points

In order to retain the material we've covered in this book, here are gleanings to consider:

- Demonstrate "unexpected friendliness" to colleagues, strangers, or casual acquaintances. In the history of religion and myth, displays of unwarranted hospitality or friendliness often prove the turning point that results in rewards being showered on someone who unknowingly aids an angel, the gods, or a disguised royal.

- Pursue topics or lines of work for which you feel zest. This is a recipe for fortuitous connections and relationships.

- Boredom is a harbinger of bad luck. Boredom leads you to rash or frivolous actions in pursuit of relief and excitement. Stay busy and engaged.

- Generosity is almost always rewarded one way or another.

- Watch for "small chances" to accomplish your aims. A small step either in conjunction with other small steps or by itself can produce unexpected results.

- Stay alert for larger "critical chances"—be watchful.

- It is lucky to know what we want. Focus brings us right action.

- Never imagine yourself more formidable or skilled than you really are. Be realistic about your current level of abilities and where they must grow.

- Healthful self-respect keeps you out of trouble.

- Avoid hyper-competitive colleagues and acquaintances. Those who make us feel competitive easily can tempt us into unlucky displays of egotism.

- Always look for how to turn chance events into good use.

- William James wrote: "A single successful effort of moral volition, such as saying 'no' to some habitual temptation, or performing some courageous act, will launch a man on a higher level of energy for days or weeks, will give him a new range of power."

- Prejudice brings bad luck.

- Ethical courage, not impulsiveness or truculence, imbues you with nobility. Defending a loved one is almost always a lucky act.

- Acting without integrity invites misfortune.

- Envy moves you to foolish actions and pettiness. It is the bug zapper of good luck.

- Any effort we make, however slight, to prevent the dictation of our behavior by insecurity feelings is a step toward luckiness.

ABOUT THE AUTHORS

Born in Chicago in 1902, A.H.Z. CARR was an economic adviser to the presidential administrations of Franklin Roosevelt and Harry Truman, and participated in economic and diplomatic missions in Western Europe and East Asia. He also served as a consulting economist to several large corporations. Carr wrote for magazines including *Harper's, Reader's Digest*, and *The Saturday Evening Post*. He died in 1971.

MITCH HOROWITZ, who abridged and introduced this volume, is the PEN Award-winning author of books including *Occult America* and *The Miracle Club: How Thoughts Become Reality*. *The Washington Post* says Mitch "treats esoteric ideas and movements with an even-handed intellectual studiousness that is too often lost in today's raised-voice discussions." Follow him @MitchHorowitz.

THE POWER
OF
CONCENTRATION

THE POWER OF CONCENTRATION

by Theron Q. Dumont

*The Classic to Harnessing
Your Mental Power*

From the Immortal Author of
The Kybalion

Abridged and Introduced
by Mitch Horowitz

THE CONDENSED CLASSICS LIBRARY™

Contents

The Voice of a Pioneer

I f you're an avid reader of metaphysical books, as I am, you might find the voice in this valuable little volume, published in 1916, somewhat familiar.

It belongs to the remarkably energetic New Thought philosopher and publisher William Walker Atkinson, who wrote under several pseudonyms and produced nearly one hundred New Thought books in the three decades leading up to his death in 1932. The most popular of these works was *The Kybalion*, which Atkinson wrote under the name "Three Initiates" in 1908, eight years before this similarly enduring volume.

In *The Power of Concentration*, Atkinson used the name French name of Theron Q. Dumont, which was often his chosen byline to explore matters of psychology, willpower, suggestion, and self-hypnosis, all of which were closely associated with French thinkers in the early twentieth century. This was particularly the case with hypnosis, which was introduced in its earliest form in Paris in the late 1770s by occult healer Franz Anton Mesmer. Although the arrival of the France Revolution, and the ensuing years of social upheaval, interrupted the progress of hypnotic theory in France, the nation once more popularized the therapeutic uses of the craft in the late-nineteenth century through the so-called Nancy School of hypnotism, which promoted practices of suggestion and hypnotherapy. The Nancy movement produced the immensely popular French healer Emile Coué, who became famous in Europe and America in the 1910s and 20s for his self-help mantra, "Day by day, in every way, I am getting better and better."

This was the tradition to which Atkinson sought to attach himself with his persona Theron Q. Dumont. Under the name Dumont, he wrote several works on the power of personal magnetism, the uses of will and suggestion, and the self-shaping forces of the mind, of which *The Power of Concentration* is probably the most compelling, persuasive, and enduring.

As is often the case with Atkinson's works, the book is a feast of practicality and idealism. It is at once inspiring and hard-knuckled—there is no toleration for dreamy visualizations unmoored from outer action. Rather, *The Power of Concentration* shows how to harness your thoughts and habits to heighten your personal performance. Nearly every page contains injunctions to act, do, and strive.

The book's advice, reduced to its essentials in this condensation, remains potent and fresh more than a century after its publication. Atkinson's language often prefigures terms and concepts heard today in the fields of neuroplasticity and cognitive behavioral therapy. Yet his book contains an infectious dynamism and scale of purpose rarely found in either of those fields. The book captures both the epic hopes and the applicability of the early days of New Thought. Its techniques have never been eclipsed or surpassed.

—Mitch Horowitz

We all know that in order to accomplish a certain thing we must concentrate. It is of the utmost value to learn how to concentrate. To make a success of anything, you must be able to concentrate your entire thought upon the idea.

Do not become discouraged if you are unable to hold your thought on the subject very long at first. Very few can. It seems a peculiar fact that it is easier to concentrate on something that is *not* good for us than on something that is beneficial. This tendency is overcome when we learn to concentrate consciously.

Did you ever stop to think what an important part your thoughts play in your life? This book shows their far-reaching and all-abiding effects.

Man is a wonderful creature, but requires training and development to be useful. A great work can be accomplished by every man if he can be awakened to do his very best. But the greatest man would accomplish little if he lacked concentration and effort. Dwarfs can do the work of giants when they are transformed by the almost-magical power of great mental concentration. But giants will only do the work of dwarfs when they lack this power.

We accomplish more by concentration than by fitness; the man that is apparently best suited for a place does not always fill it best. It is the man who concentrates on every possibility that makes an art of both his work, and his life.

This course will stimulate and inspire you to achieve success; it will bring you into perfect harmony with the laws of success. It will give you a firmer hold on your duties and responsibilities.

The methods of thought-concentration given in this work, if put into practice, will open up interior avenues that will connect you with the everlasting laws of Being and their exhaustless foundation of unchangeable truth.

Concentration Finds the Way

E veryone has two natures. One wants to advance and the other wants to pull back. The one that we cultivate and concentrate on decides what we are at the end. Both natures are vying for control. The will alone decides the issue. A man by one supreme effort of the will may change his whole career, and almost accomplish miracles. You may be that man. You can be if you Will to be, for Will can find a way, or make one.

It is a matter of choice whether we allow our diviner self to control us, or whether we get controlled by the brute within. No man has to do anything he does not want to do. He is therefore the director of his life, if he wills to be. What we do is the result of our training. We are like putty, and can be completely controlled by our willpower.

Many people read good books, but say they do not get much out of them. They do not realize that all any book or lesson can do is to awaken them to their possibilities. One of the most beneficial practices I know of is looking for the good in everyone and everything, for there is good in all things. We encourage a person by seeing his good qualities, and we also help ourselves by looking for them. We gain their good wishes, a most valuable asset. We get back what we give out. The time comes when most all of us need encouragement; need buoying up. So, form the habit of encouraging others, and you will find it a wonderful tonic for both others and yourself, for you will get back encouraging and uplifting thoughts.

The first of each month, a person should sit down and examine the progress he has made. If he has not come up to expectations he should discover the reason, and by extra exertion measure up to what is demanded.

I know that every man who is willing to pay the price can be a success. The price is not in money, but in effort. The first essential quality for success is the desire to do—*to be something*. The next thing is to learn how to do it; the next to carry it into execution. The man best able to accomplish anything is the one with a broad mind; a man may acquire knowledge that is foreign to a particular case, but is, nevertheless, of some value in all cases. So, the man who wants to be successful must be liberal; he must acquire all the knowledge he can; he must be well posted not only in one branch of his business but in every part of it. Such a man achieves success.

The secret of success is to try always to improve yourself no matter where you are or what your position. Learn all you can. Don't see how little you can do, but how much you can do. Such a man will always be in demand.

The man with grit and will may be poor today and wealthy in a few years; willpower is a better asset than money. Will will carry you over chasms of failure, if you but give it the chance.

Everyone *really wants* to do something, but few will put forward the effort to make the necessary sacrifice to secure it. There is only one way to accomplish anything, and that is to go ahead and do it. A man may accomplish almost anything today, if he just sets his heart on it and lets nothing interfere with his progress. Obstacles are quickly overcome by the man that sets out to accomplish his heart's desire. The "bigger" the man, the smaller the obstacle appears. The "smaller" the man the greater the obstacle appears. Always look at the advantage you gain by overcoming obstacles, and it will give you the needed courage for their conquest.

The Self-Mastery
Power of Concentration

Man from a psychological standpoint of development is not what he should be. He does not possess the self-mastery, the self-directing power of concentration that is his right.

He has not trained himself to promote his self-mastery. Every balanced mind possesses faculties whose chief duties are to engineer, direct, and concentrate the operations of the mind, both in a mental and physical sense. Man must learn to control not only his mind but also his bodily movements.

When the self-regulating faculties are not developed the impulses, appetites, emotions, and passions have full swing, and the mind becomes impulsive, restless, emotional, and irregular. This makes mental concentration poor.

When the self-guiding faculties are weak, the person always lacks the power of mental concentration. Therefore, you cannot concentrate until you develop those very powers that *qualify* you to concentrate. If you cannot concentrate, one of the following is the cause:

1. Deficiency of the motor centers.
2. An impulsive and emotional mind.
3. An untrained mind.

The last fault can soon be removed by systematic practice. It is easiest to correct.

The impulsive and emotional state of mind can best be corrected by restraining anger, passion and excitement, hatred, strong impulses, intense emotions, fretfulness, etc. It is impossible to concentrate when you are in any of these excited states. You can help naturally decrease these by avoiding food and drinks as have nerve weakening or stimulating influences, or a tendency to stir up the passions, impulses, and emotions. It is also a good practice to watch and associate with people who are steady, calm, controlled, and conservative.

Many have the idea that when they get into a negative state they are concentrating, but this is not so. Their power of concentration becomes weaker, and they find it difficult to concentrate on anything. The mind that cannot center itself on a special subject or thought, is weak; as is the mind that cannot draw itself from a subject or thought. But the person who can center his mind on any problem, no matter what it is, and remove any unharmonious impressions, has strength of mind. Concentration, first, last, and all the time, means strength of mind.

A concentrated mind pays attention to thoughts, words, acts, and plans. The person who allows his mind to roam at will, will never accomplish a great deal in the world. He wastes his energies. You concentrate the moment you say, "I want to, I can, I will."

Concentration of the mind can only be developed by watching yourself closely. All kinds of development commence with close attention. You should regulate your every thought and feeling. When you commence to watch yourself, your own acts, and also the acts of other people, you use the faculties of autonomy, and, as you continue to do so, you improve your faculties, until in time you can engineer your every thought, wish, and plan. Only the trained mind can focalize. To hold a thought before it until all the faculties have had time to consider that thought is concentration.

The person who cannot direct his thoughts, wishes, plans, resolutions, and studies cannot possibly succeed to the fullest extent. The person who is impulsive one moment and calm the next has not the proper control over himself. He is not a master of his mind, nor of his thoughts, feelings, and wishes. Such a person cannot be a success. When he becomes irritated, he irritates others and spoils all chances of any concerned doing their best. But the person who can direct his energies and hold them at work in a concentrated manner controls his every work and act, and thereby gains power to control others. He can make his every move serve a useful end, and every thought a noble purpose.

He is consciously attentive and holds his mind to one thing at a time. He shuts out everything else. When you are talking to anyone give him your sole and undivided attention. Do not let your attention wander or be diverted. Give no heed to anything else, but make your will and intellect act in unison.

Start out in the morning and see how self-poised you can remain all day. At times, take an inventory of your actions during the day and see if you have kept your determination. If not, see that you do tomorrow. The more self-poised you are the better your concentration. Never be in too much of a hurry; and, remember, the more you improve your concentration, the greater are your possibilities. Concentration means success, because you are better able to govern yourself and centralize your mind; you become more in earnest in what you do, and this almost invariably improves your chances for success.

When you are talking to a person have your own plans in mind. Concentrate your strength upon the purpose you are talking about. Watch his every move, but keep your own plans before you. Unless you do, you will waste your energy and not accomplish as much as you should.

I want you to watch the next person you see who has the reputation of being a strong character, a man of force. Watch and see what a perfect control he has over his body. Then I want you to watch just an ordinary person. Notice how he moves his eyes, arms, fingers; notice the useless expenditure of energy. These movements lessen the person's power in vital and nerve directions. Center your mind on one purpose, one plan, one transaction.

There is nothing that uses up nerve force so quickly as excitement. This is why an irritable person is never magnetic; he is never admired or loved; he does not develop those finer qualities that a real gentleman possesses. Anger, sarcasm, and excitement weaken a person in this direction. The person that allows himself to get excited will become nervous in time, because he uses up his nerve forces and his vital energies. The person that cannot control himself and keep from becoming excited cannot concentrate.

But those whose actions are slower and directed by their intelligence develop concentration. Sometimes dogmatic, willful, excitable persons can concentrate, but it is spasmodic, erratic concentration instead of controlled and uniform concentration. Their energy works by spells; sometimes they have plenty, other times very little; it is easily excited; easily wasted. The best way to understand it is to compare it with the discharge of a gun. If the gun goes off when you want it to, it accomplishes the purpose, but if it goes off before you are ready, you not only waste ammunition, but are also likely to do some damage. That is just what most people do. They allow their energy to explode, thus not only wasting it, but also endangering others. They waste their power, their magnetism, and so injure their chance of success.

The brain is the storehouse of the energy. Most all persons have all the dynamic energy they need if they would concentrate it. They have the machine, but they must also have the engineer, or they will not go very far. The engineer is the self-regulating, directing power. The good engineer controls his every act. By what you do you either advance or degenerate. This is a good idea to keep always in mind. When you are uncertain whether you should do something, just think whether by doing it you will grow or deteriorate, and act accordingly.

I am a firm believer in "work when you work, play when you play." When you give yourself up to pleasure you can develop concentration by thinking of nothing else but pleasure; when your mind dwells on love, think of nothing but this and you will find you can develop a more intense love than you ever had before. When you concentrate your mind on the "you" or real self, and its wonderful possibilities, you develop concentration and a higher opinion of yourself. By doing this systematically, you develop power, because you cannot be systematic without concentrating on what you are doing. When you walk out into the country and inhale the fresh air, studying vegetation, trees, etc., you are concentrating. Whenever you fix your mind on a certain thought and hold your mind on it at successive intervals, you develop concentration.

If you hold your mind on some chosen object, you centralize your attention, just like the lens of the camera centralizes on a certain landscape. Therefore, always hold your mind on what you are doing, no matter what it is.

Practice inhaling long, deep breaths, not simply for the improvement of health, although that is no small matter, but also for the purpose of developing more power, more love, more life. All work assists in development.

If you want to get more out of life you must think more of love. Unless you have real affection for something, you have no sentiment, no sweetness, no magnetism. So arouse your love affections by your will, and enter into a fuller life.

The next time you feel yourself becoming irritable, use your will and be patient. This is a very good exercise in self-control. It will help you to keep patient if you will breathe slowly and deeply. If you find you are commencing to speak fast, just control yourself and speak slowly and clearly. Keep from either raising or lowering your voice, and concentrate on the fact that you are determined to keep your poise, and you will improve your power of concentration.

If you feel yourself getting irritable, nervous or weak, stand squarely on your feet with your chest up and inhale deeply, and you will see that your irritability will disappear and a silent calm will pass over you.

If you are in the habit of associating with nervous, irritable people, quit it until you grow strong in the power of concentration, because irritable, angry, fretful, dogmatic, and disagreeable people will weaken what powers of resistance you have.

When your eye is steady, your mind is steady. One of the best ways to study a person is to watch his physical movements, for, when we study his actions, we are studying his mind. Because actions are the expressions of the mind. As the mind is, so is the action. When you learn to control the body, you are gaining control over the mind.

How to Gain What You Want Through Concentration

The ignorant person may say, "How can you get anything by merely wanting it?" I say that through concentration you can get anything you want. Every desire can be gratified. But whether it is, will depend upon you concentrating to have that desire fulfilled. Merely wishing for something will not bring it. Wishing you had something shows a weakness, and not a belief that you will really get it. So never merely wish, as we are not living in a "fairy age." You use up just as much brain force in "vain imaginings" as you do when you think of something worthwhile.

Be careful of your desires, make a mental picture of what you want and set your will to this until it materializes. Never allow yourself to drift without helm or rudder. Know what you want to do, and strive with all your might to do it, and you will succeed.

Feel that you can accomplish anything you undertake. Many undertake to do things, but feel when they start they are going to fail, and usually they do. I will give an illustration. A man goes to a store for an article. The clerk says, "I am sorry, we do not have it." But the man that is determined to get that thing inquires if he doesn't know where he can get it. Again receiving an unsatisfactory answer the determined buyer consults the manager, and finally finds where the article can be bought.

That is the whole secret of concentrating on getting what you want. And, remember, your soul is a center of all-power, and you can accomplish what you will to. "I'll find a way or make one!" is the spirit that wins. I know a man who is now head of a large bank. He started there as a messenger boy. His father had a button made for him with a "P" on it and put it on his coat. He said, "Son, that 'P' is a reminder that some day you are to be the president of your bank. I want you to keep this thought in your mind. Every day do something that will put you nearer your goal." Each night after supper he would say, "Son, what did you do today?" In this way the thought was always kept in mind. He concentrated on becoming president of that bank, and he did. His father told him never to tell anyone what that "P" stood for. His associates made a good deal of fun of it. And they tried to find out what it stood for, but they never did until he was made president, and then he told the secret.

Don't waste your mental powers in wishes. Don't dissipate your energies by trying to satisfy every whim. Concentrate on doing something really worthwhile. The man that sticks to something is not the man that fails.

"Power to him who power exerts."
—EMERSON

This great universe is interwoven with myriad forces. You make your own place, and whether it is important depends upon you. Through the Indestructible and Unconquerable Law you can, in time, accomplish all right things, and therefore do not be afraid to undertake whatever you really desire to accomplish and are willing to pay for in effort. *Anything that is right is possible.* That which is necessary will inevitably take place. If something is right, it is your duty to do it, though the whole world thinks it to be wrong.

"God and one are always a majority," or in plain words, that omnipotent interior law which is God, and the organism that represents you, is able to conquer the whole world if your cause is absolutely just. Don't say, "I wish I were great." You can do anything that is proper, and that you want to. Just say: You can. You will. You must. *Realize this* and the rest is easy.

The Silent Force That Produces Results

Through concentrated thought power you can make yourself whatever you please. By thought you can greatly increase your efficiency and strength. You are surrounded by all kinds of thoughts, some good, others bad, and you are sure to absorb some of the latter if you do not build up a positive mental attitude.

If you will study the needless moods of anxiety, worry, despondency, discouragement, and others that are the result of uncontrolled thoughts, you will realize how important the control of your thoughts are. Your thoughts make you what you are.

When I walk along the street and study the different people's faces I can tell how they spent their lives. It all shows in their faces, just like a mirror reflects their physical countenances. In looking in those faces I cannot help thinking how most of the people you see have wasted their lives.

Understanding the power of thought will awaken possibilities within you that you never dreamed of. Never forget that your thoughts are making your environment and your friends, and as your thoughts change these will also. The desire to do right carries with it a great power. I want you to thoroughly realize the importance of your thoughts, and how to make them valuable, to understand that your thoughts come to you over invisible wires and influence you.

In order to speak wisely you must secure at least a partial concentration of the faculties and forces upon the subject at hand. Speech interferes with the focusing powers of the mind, as it withdraws the attention to the external and therefore is hardly to be compared with that deep silence of the subconscious mind, where deep thoughts, and the silent forces of high potency, are evolved. It is necessary to be silent before you can speak wisely. The person who is really alert, well poised, and able to speak wisely under trying circumstances, is the person who has practiced in the silence. Most people do not know what the silence is and think it is easy to go into the silence, but this is not so. In the real silence, we become attached to that interior law and the forces become silent, because they are in a state of high potency. Hold the thought: In-silence-I-will-allow-my-higher-self-to-have-complete-control. I-will-be-true-to-my-higher-self. I-will-live-true-to-my-conception-of-what-is-right. I-realize-that-it-is-in-my-self-interest-to-live-up-to-my-best. I-demand-wisdom-so-that-I-may-act-wisely-for-myself-and-others.

In the next chapter, I tell you of the mysterious law that links all humanity together by the powers of co-operative thought, and chooses for us companionship and friends.

How Concentrated Thought Links All Humanity

Success is the result of how you think. I will show you how to think to be successful.

The power to rule and attract success is within yourself. The barriers that shut these off from you are subject to your control. You have unlimited power to think, and this is the link that connects you with your omniscient source.

Success is the result of certain moods of mind or ways of thinking. These moods can be controlled by you, and produced at will.

Concentrated thought will accomplish seemingly impossible results and make you realize your fondest ambitions. At the same time that you break down barriers of limitation new ambitions will be awakened. If you will just realize that through deep concentration you become linked with thoughts of omnipotence, you will kill out entirely your belief in your limitations, and at the same time will drive away all fear and other negative and destructive thought forces, which constantly work against you.

It is just as easy to surround your life with what you want as it is with what you don't. It is a question to be decided by your will. There are no walls to prevent you from getting what you want, *providing you want what is right*. If you choose something that is not right, you are in opposition to the omnipotent plans of the universe, and deserve to fail. *But, if you base your desires on justice and good will, you avail yourself of the helpful powers of universal currents, and instead of having a handicap to work against, can depend upon ultimate success, though the outward appearances may not at first be bright.*

Never stop to think of temporary appearances, but maintain an unfaltering belief in your ultimate success. Make your plans carefully, and see that they are not contrary to the tides of universal justice. The main thing for you to remember is to keep at bay the destructive and opposing forces of fear, anger, and their satellites.

There is no power so great as the belief which comes from the knowledge that your thought is in harmony with the divine laws of thought, and the sincere conviction that your cause is right.

All just causes succeed in time, though temporarily they may fail. So if you should face the time when everything seems against you, quiet your fears, drive away all destructive thoughts, and uphold the dignity of your moral and spiritual life.

The following method may assist you in gaining better thought control. If you are unable to control your fears, just say to your faulty determination, "Do not falter or be afraid, for I am not really alone. I am surrounded by invisible forces that will assist me to remove the unfavorable appearances." Soon you will have more courage. The only difference between the fearless man and the fearful one is in his will, his hope. So if you lack success, believe in it, hope for it, claim it. You can use the same method to brace up your thoughts of desire, aspiration, imagination, expectation, ambition, understanding, trust, and assurance.

If you get anxious, angry, discouraged, undecided or worried, it is because you are not receiving the cooperation of the higher powers of your mind. By your Will you can so organize the powers of the mind that your moods change only as you want them to instead of as circumstances affect you. If you allow the mind to wander while you are doing small things, it will be likely to get into mischief and make it hard to concentrate on the important act when it comes.

The will does not act with clearness, decision and promptness *unless it is trained to do so.* Comparatively few people really know what they are doing every minute of the day. This is because they do not observe with sufficient orderliness and accuracy. It is not difficult to know what you are doing all the time, if you will just practice concentration, and with a reposeful deliberation train yourself to think clearly, promptly, and decisively.

If you allow yourself to worry or hurry in what you are doing, it will not be clearly photographed upon the sensitized plate of the subjective mind, and therefore you will not be really conscious of your actions. So practice accuracy and concentration of thought, and also absolute truthfulness, and you will soon be able to concentrate.

The Training of the Will to Do

The Will To Do is the greatest power in the world that is concerned with human accomplishment, and no one can predetermine its limits.

The Will To Do is a force that is strictly practical, yet it is difficult to explain just what it is. It can be compared to electricity because we know it only through its cause and effects. Every time you accomplish any definite act, consciously or unconsciously, you use the principle of the Will. You can Will to do anything, whether right or wrong, and therefore how you use your will makes a big difference in your life.

Every person possesses some "Will To Do." It is the inner energy that controls all conscious acts. *Genius is but a will to do little things with infinite pains. Little things done well open the door of opportunity for bigger things.*

Study yourself carefully. Find out your greatest weakness and then use your willpower to overcome it.

In this way eradicate your faults, one by one, until you have built up a strong character and personality.

Rules for Improvement. A desire arises. Now think whether this would be good for you. If it is not, use your Willpower to kill out the desire; but, on the other hand, if it is a righteous desire, summon all your Willpower to your aid, crush all obstacles that confront you, and secure possession of the coveted Good.

Slowness in Making Decisions. This is a weakness of Willpower. You know you should do something, but you delay doing it through lack of decision. It is easier not to do a certain thing , but conscience says to do it. The vast majority of people are failures because of the lack of deciding to do a thing when it should be done. Those that are successful have been quick to grasp opportunities by making a quick decision. This power of will can be used to bring culture, wealth, and health.

Some Special Pointers. For the next week try to make quicker decisions in your little daily affairs. Set the hour you wish to get up and arise exactly at the fixed time. Anything that you should accomplish, do on or ahead of time. You want, of course, to give due deliberation to weighty matters, but by making quick decisions on little things you will acquire the ability to make quick decisions in bigger things.

You Are as Good as Anyone. You have willpower, and if you use it, you will get your share of the luxuries of life. So use it to claim your own. Don't depend on anyone else to help you. We have to fight our own battles. All the world loves a fighter, while the coward is despised by all. Every person's problems are different, so I can only say "analyze your opportunities and conditions and study your natural abilities." Don't make an indefinite plan, but a definite one, and then don't give up until your object has been accomplished. Put these suggestions into practice with true earnestness, and you will soon note astonishing results, and your whole life will be completely changed. An excellent motto for one of pure motives is: *Through my willpower I dare do what I want to.* You will find this affirmation has a very strengthening effect.

The Spirit of Perseverance. The spirit of "stick-toitiveness" is the one that wins. Many go just so far and then give up, whereas, if they had persevered a little longer, they would have won out. Many have much initiative, but instead of concentrating it into one channel they diffuse it through several, thereby dissipating it to such an extent that its effect is lost.

Lack of Perseverance is nothing but the lack of the Will To Do. It takes the same energy to say, "I will continue," as to say, "I give up." Just the moment you say the latter you shut off your dynamo, and your determination is gone. Every time you allow your determination to be broken you weaken it. Don't forget this. Just the instant you notice your determination beginning to weaken, concentrate on it and by sheer Will Power make it continue on the "job."

Never try to make a decision when you are not in a calm state of mind. If in a "quick temper," you are likely to say things you regret. In anger, you follow impulse rather than reason. No one can expect to achieve success if he makes decisions when not in full control of his mental forces. Therefore make it a fixed rule to make decisions only when at your best.

Special Instructions to Develop the Will To Do. This is a form of mental energy, but requires the proper mental attitude to make it manifest. We hear of people having wonderful willpower, which really is wrong. It should be said that they *use* their willpower, while with many it is a latent force. I want you to realize that no one has a monopoly on willpower. What we speak of as willpower is but the gathering together of mental energy, the concentration of power at one point. So never think of someone as having a stronger will than you. Each person will be supplied with just that amount of willpower that he demands.

The Concentrated Mental Demand

The Mental Demand is the potent force in achievement. The attitude of the mind affects the expression of the face, determines action, changes our physical condition, and regulates our lives.

The mental demand must be directed by every power of the mind, and every possible element should be used to make the demand materialize. You can so intently desire a thing that you can exclude all distracting thoughts. When you practice this singleness of concentration until you attain the end sought, you have developed a Will capable of accomplishing whatever you wish.

The men looked upon as the world's successes have not always been men of great physical power, nor at the start did they seem very well adapted to the conditions around them. In the beginning, they were not considered men of superior genius, but they won their success by their resolution to achieve results by permitting no setback to dishearten them; no difficulties to daunt them. Nothing could turn them or influence them against their determination. They never lost sight of their goal. In all of us there is this silent force of wonderful power. If developed, it can overcome conditions that would seem insurmountable. It is constantly urging us on to greater achievement. The more we become acquainted with it the better strategists we become, the more courage we develop, and the greater the desire within us for self-expression along many lines.

No one will ever be a failure if he becomes conscious of this silent force within that controls his destiny. But without the consciousness of this inner force, you will not have a clear vision, and external conditions will not yield to the power of your mind. It is the mental resolve that makes achievement possible. Once this has been formed it should never be allowed to cease to press its claim until its object is attained.

Perseverance is the first element of success. In order to persevere you must be ceaseless in your application. It requires you to concentrate your thoughts upon your undertaking, and bring every energy to bear upon keeping them focused upon it until you have accomplished your aim. To quit short of this is to weaken all future efforts.

The Mental Demand seems an unreal power because it is intangible; but it is the mightiest power in the world. It is a power that is free for you to use. No one can use it for you. Every time you make a Mental Demand you strengthen the brain centers by drawing to you external forces.

Few realize the power of a Mental Demand. It is possible to make your demand so strong that you can impart what you have to say to another without speaking to him. Have you ever, after planning to discuss a certain matter with a friend, had the experience of having him broach the subject before you had a chance to speak of it? These things are neither coincidences nor accidents, but are the results of mental demand launched by strong concentration. The person that never wants anything gets little. To demand resolutely is the first step toward getting what you want.

Once the Mental Demand is made, however, never let it falter. If you do, the current that connects you with your desire is broken. Take all the necessary time to build a firm foundation, so that there need not be even an element of doubt to creep in. Just the moment you entertain "doubt" you lose some of the demand force, and force once lost is hard to regain. So whenever you make a mental demand hold steadfastly to it until your need is supplied.

And every man of AVERAGE ability, the ordinary man that you see about you, can be really successful, independent, free of worry, HIS OWN MASTER, if he can manage to do just two things: First, remain forever dissatisfied with what he IS doing and with what he HAS accomplished. Second, develop in his mind a belief that the word "impossible" was not intended for him. Build up in his mind the confidence that enables the mind to use its power.

Concentration Gives Mental Poise

You will find that the man that concentrates is well poised, whereas the man that allows his mind to wander is easily upset. When in this state wisdom does not pass from the subconscious store-house into the consciousness. There must be mental quiet before the two forms of consciousness can work in harmony. When you are able to concentrate, you have peace of mind.

If you are in the habit of losing your poise, form the habit of reading literature that has a quieting power. Just the second you feel your poise slipping, say, "Peace," and then hold this thought in mind and you will never lose your self-control. Think of yourself as a child of the infinite, possessing infinite possibilities. Write on a piece of paper, "I have the power to do and to be whatever I wish to do and be." Keep this mentally before you, and you will find the thought will be of great help to you.

The Mistake of Concentrating on Your Business While Away. In order to be successful today, you must concentrate, but don't become a slave to concentration, and carry your business cares home. Just as sure as you do, you will be burning the life forces at both ends, and the fire will go out much sooner than intended.

Many men become so absorbed in their business that when they go to church they do not hear the preacher because their minds are on their business. If they go to the theater they do not enjoy it because their business is on their minds. When they go to bed they think about business instead of sleep. This is the wrong kind of concentration and is dangerous. It is involuntary. It is a big mistake to let a thought rule you, instead of ruling it. He who does not rule himself is not a success. If you cannot control your concentration, your health will suffer.

Never become so absorbed with anything that you cannot lay it aside and take up another. This is self-control. Concentration is paying attention to a chosen thought.

Self-Study Valuable. Everyone has some habits that can be overcome by concentration. We will say for instance, you are in the habit of complaining, or finding fault with yourself or others; or, imagining that you do not possess the ability of others; or feeling that you are not as good as someone else; or that you cannot rely on yourself; or harboring any similar thoughts. These should be cast aside, and instead thoughts of strength should be put in their place. Just remember that every time you think of yourself as being weak, in some way you are making yourself so. Our mental conditions make us what we are. Just watch yourself and see how much time you waste in worrying, fretting, and complaining. The more of it you do, the worse off you are.

Just the minute you are aware of thinking a negative thought immediately change to a positive one. If you start to think of failure, change to thinking of success. You have the germ of success within you. Care for it the same as the setting hen broods over the eggs, and you can make it a reality.

You can make those that you come in contact with feel as you do, because you radiate vibrations of the way you feel, and your vibrations are felt by others. When you concentrate on a certain thing you turn all the rays of your vibrations on this. Thought is the directing power of all Life's vibrations. If a person should enter a room with a lot of people and feel as if he were a person of no consequence, no one would know he was there unless they saw him; and even if they did, they would not remember seeing him, because they were not attracted towards him. But let him enter the room feeling that he was magnetic and concentrating on this thought, others would feel his vibration. So remember, the way you feel you can make others feel.

If you will study all of the great characters of history you will find that they were enthusiastic. First, they were enthusiastic themselves, and then they could arouse others' enthusiasm. It is latent in everyone. It is a wonderful force when once aroused. This is the keynote of success.

"Think, speak, and act just as you wish to be, And you will be that which you wish to be."

You are just what you think you are, and not what you may appear to be. You may fool others, but not yourself. You may control your life and actions just as you can control your hands. If you want to raise your hand, you must first think of raising it. If you want to control your life, you must first control your thinking. Easy to do, is it not? Yes it is, if you will but concentrate on what you think about.

How can we secure concentration? To this question, the first and last answer must be: by interest and strong motive. The stronger the motive, the greater the concentration.

Successful Lives Are the Concentrated Lives.
Train yourself so that you will be able to centralize
your thought, develop your brainpower, and increase
your mental energy, or you can be a slacker, a drifter,
a quitter, or a sleeper. It all depends on how you concentrate, or centralize your thoughts. Your thinking
then becomes a fixed power and you do not waste time
thinking about something that would not be good for
you. You pick out the thoughts that will be the means
of bringing you what you desire, and they become a material reality. Whatever we create in the thought world
will some day materialize. That is the law. Never forget
this.

**Why People Often Do Not Get What They Con-
centrate On.** Because they sit down in hopeless despair
and expect it to come to them. But if they will just reach
out for it with their biggest effort they will find it is
within their reach. No one limits us but ourselves.

Through our concentration we can attract what we
want, because we became en rapport with the Universal
forces, from which we can get what we want.

A man starts to think on a certain subject. He has
all kinds of thoughts come to him, but by concentration
he shuts out all these but the one he has chosen. Concentration is just a case of willing to do a certain thing,
and doing it.

If you want to accomplish anything, first put yourself in a concentrating, reposeful, receptive, acquiring frame of mind. In tackling unfamiliar work make haste slowly and deliberately, and then you will secure that interior activity, which is never possible when you are in a hurry or under a strain. When you "think hard," or try to hurry results too quickly, you generally shut off the interior flow of thoughts and ideas. You have often no doubt tried hard to think of something but could not, but just as soon as you stopped trying to think of it, it came to you.

Concentration Can Overcome Bad Habits

Habits make or break us to a far greater extent than we like to admit. Habit is both a powerful enemy and wonderful ally of concentration. You must learn to overcome habits that are injurious to concentration, and to cultivate those that increase it.

Most people are controlled by their habits, and are buffeted around by them like waves of the ocean tossing a piece of wood. They do things in a certain way because of the power of habit. They seldom ever think of concentrating on why they do them this or that way, or study to see if they could do them in a better way.

The first thing I want you to realize is that all habits are governed consciously or unconsciously by the will. Most of us are forming new habits all the time. Very often, if you repeat something several times in the same way, you will have formed the habit of doing it that way. But the oftener you repeat it the stronger that habit grows, and the more deeply it becomes embedded in your nature. After a habit has been in force for a long time, it becomes almost a part of you, and is therefore hard to overcome. But you can still break any habit by strong concentration on its opposite.

You will find the following maxims worth remembering.

First Maxim: "We must make our nervous system our ally instead of our enemy."

Second Maxim: "In the acquisition of a new habit as in the leaving off of an old one, we must take care to launch ourselves with as strong and decided an initiative as possible."

Surround yourself with every aid you can. Don't play with fire by forming bad habits. Make a new beginning today. Study why you have been doing certain things. If they are not for your good, shun them henceforth. Don't give in to a single temptation, for every time you do, you strengthen the chain of bad habits. Every time you keep a resolution you break the chain that enslaves you.

Third Maxim: "Never allow an exception to occur till the new habit is securely rooted in your life."

Fourth Maxim: "Seize the very first possible opportunity to act on every resolution you make, and on every emotional prompting you may experience in the direction of the habits you aspire to gain."

Keep every resolution you make, for you not only profit by the resolution, but it furnishes you with an exercise that causes the brain cells and physiological correlatives to form the habit of adjusting themselves to carry out resolutions. A tendency to act becomes effectively engrained in us in proportion to the uninterrupted frequency with which the actions actually occur, and the brain "grows" to their use.

Fifth Maxim: "Keep the faculty of effort alive in you by a little gratuitous exercise every day."

The more we exercise the will, the better we can control our habits. Every few days, do something for no other reason than its difficulty, so that when the hour of dire need draws near, it may find you not unnerved or untrained to stand the test. Asceticism of this sort is like the insurance that a man pays on his house and goods. So with the man who has daily insured himself to habits of concentrated attention, energetic volition, and self-denial in unnecessary things.

Habits have often been called a labor-saving invention, because when they are formed they require less of both mental and material strength. The more deeply the habit becomes ingrained, the more automatic it becomes. Therefore habit is an economizing tendency of our nature, for if it were not for habit we should have to be more watchful. We walk across a crowded street; the habit of stopping and looking prevents us from being hurt. Habits mean less risk, less fatigue, and greater accuracy.

In order to overcome undesirable habits, two things are necessary. You must have trained your will to do what you want it to do, and the stronger the will the easier it will be to break a habit. Then you must make a resolution to do just the opposite of what the habit is. I will bring this chapter to a close by giving Doctor Oppenheim's instructions for overcoming a habit:

"If you want to abolish a habit, and its accumulated circumstances as well, you must grapple with the matter as earnestly as you would with a physical enemy. You must go into the encounter with all tenacity of determination, with all fierceness of resolve—and yea, even with a passion for success that may be called vindictive.

No human enemy can be as insidious, so persevering, as unrelenting as an unfavorable habit. It never sleeps, it needs no rest.

"It is like a parasite that grows with the growth of the supporting body, and, like a parasite, it can best be killed by violent separation and crushing."

It is not in the easy, contented moments of our life that we make our greatest progress, for then it requires no special effort to keep in tune. But it is when we are in the midst of trials and misfortunes, when we think we are sinking, being overwhelmed, then it is important for us to realize that we are linked to a great Power, and if we live as we should, there is nothing that can occur in life that could permanently injure us, nothing can happen that should disturb us. Always remember you have within you unlimited power, ready to manifest itself in the form which fills our need at the moment.

Business Results Through Concentration

usiness success depends on well-concentrated efforts. You must use every mental force you can master. The more these are used, the more they increase. Therefore the more you accomplish today the more force you will have at your disposal to solve your problems tomorrow. Then when you have resolved what you want to do, you will be drawn towards it. There is a law that opens the way to the fulfillment of your desires. Of course, back of your desire you must put forward the necessary effort to carry out your purpose; you must use your power to put your desires into force. Once they are created, and you keep up your determination to have them fulfilled, you both consciously and unconsciously work toward their materialization. Set your heart on your purpose, concentrate your thought upon it, direct your efforts with all your intelligence, and in due time you will realize your ambition.

Feel yourself a success, believe you are a success, and thus put yourself in the attitude that demands recognition and the thought current draws to you what you need to make you a success. Don't be afraid of big undertakings. Go at them with grit, and pursue methods that you think will accomplish your purpose. You may not at first meet with entire success, but aim so high that if you fall a little short you will still have accomplished much.

What others have done you can do. You may even do what others have been unable to do. Always keep a strong desire to succeed in your mind. Be in love with your aim and work, and make it, as far as possible, square with the rule of the greatest good to the greatest number, and your life cannot be a failure.

The successful business attitude must be cultivated to make the most out of your life: the attitude of expecting great things from both yourself and others. This alone will often cause men to make good; to measure up to the best that is in them.

It is not the spasmodic spurts that count on a long journey, but the steady efforts. Spurts fatigue, and make it hard for you to continue.

When once you reach a conclusion abide by it. Let there be no doubt, or wavering. If you are uncertain about every decision you make, you will be subject to harassing doubts and fears, which will render your judgment of little value. The man that decides according to what he thinks right, and who learns from every mistake, acquires a well-balanced mind that gets the best results. He gains the confidence of others. He is known as the man who knows what he wants, and not as one that is as changeable as the weather. Reliable firms want to do business with men of known qualities, with men of firmness, judgment, and reliability.

So, if you wish to start in business for yourself, your greatest asset, with the single exception of a sound physique, is that of a good reputation.

A successful business is not hard to build if we can concentrate all our mental forces upon it. We hear people say that business is trying on the nerves, but it is the unsettling elements of fret, worry, and suspense that are nerve exhausting, and not the business. Executing one's plans may cause fatigue, but enjoyment comes with rest. If there has not been any unnatural strain, the recuperative powers replace what energy has been lost.

By attending to each day's work properly, you develop the capacity to do a greater work tomorrow. It is this gradual development that makes possible the carrying out of big plans.

Even brilliant men's conceptions of the possibilities of their mental forces are so limited and below their real worth that they are far more likely to belittle their possibilities than they are to exaggerate them. You don't want to think that an aim is impossible because it has never been realized in the past. Everyday someone is doing something that was never done before.

The natural leader always draws to himself, by the law of mental attraction, all the ideas in his chosen subject that have ever been conceived by others. This is of the greatest importance and help. If you are properly trained you benefit much by others' thoughts, and, providing you generate from within yourself something of value, they will benefit from yours. "We are heirs of all the ages," but we must know how to use our inheritance.

The confident, pushing, hopeful, determined man influences all with whom he associates, and inspires the same qualities in them. There is no reason why your work or business should burn you out. When it does, something is wrong. You are attracting forces and influence that you should not, because you are not in harmony with what you are doing. There is nothing so tiring as trying to do work for which we are unfitted both by temperament and training.

Each one should be engaged in a business that he loves; he should be furthering movements with which he is in sympathy. Only then will he do his best, and take intense pleasure in his business. In this way, while constantly growing and developing his powers, he is at the same time rendering through his work genuine and devoted service to humanity.

Concentrate On Your Courage

Courage is the backbone of man. The man with courage has persistence. He states what he believes, and puts it into execution.

Lack of courage creates financial, as well as mental and moral difficulties. When a new problem comes, instead of looking upon it as something to be achieved, the man or woman without courage looks for reasons why it cannot be done, and failure is naturally the almost inevitable result. This is a subject well worth your study. Look upon everything within your power as a possibility, and you will accomplish a great deal more, because by considering a thing as impossible you immediately draw to yourself all the elements that contribute to failure. Lack of courage destroys your confidence in yourself.

The man without courage unconsciously draws to himself all that is contemptible, weakening, demoralizing, and destructive. We must first have the courage to *strongly desire something.* A desire to be fulfilled must be backed by the strength of all our mental forces. Such a desire has enough commanding force to change all unfavorable conditions.

What is courage? It is the *Will To Do.* It takes no more energy to be courageous than to be cowardly. It is a matter of the right training, in the right way. Courage concentrates the mental forces on the task at hand. It then directs them thoughtfully, steadily, deliberately, while attracting all the forces of success toward the desired end.

As we are creatures of habits, we should avoid people who lack courage. They are easy to discover because of their habits of fear in attacking new problems. The man with courage is never afraid.

Start out today with the idea that there is no reason why you should not be courageous. If any fear-thoughts come to you, cast them off as you would the deadly viper. Form the habit of never thinking of anything unfavorable to yourself or anyone else. In dealing with difficulties, new or old, hold ever the thought: "I am courageous." Whenever a doubt crosses the threshold of your mind, banish it. Remember, you as master of your mind control its every thought, and here is a good one to often affirm: "I have courage because I desire it;

because I need it; because I use it; and because I refuse to become such a weakling as cowardice produces."

There is no justification for the loss of courage. The evils by which you will almost certainly be overwhelmed without it are far greater than those which courage will help you to meet and overcome. Right, then, must be the moralist who says that the only thing to fear is fear.

Never let another's opinion affect you; he cannot tell what you are able to do; he does not know what you can do with your forces. The truth is, you do not know yourself until you put yourself to the test. Therefore, how can someone else know? Never let anyone else put a valuation on you.

Almost all wonderful achievements have been accomplished after it had been "thoroughly" demonstrated that they were impossibilities. Once we understand the law, all things are possible. If they were impossibilities, we could not conceive them.

Just the moment you allow someone to influence you against what you think is right, you lose that confidence that inspires courage and carries with it all the forces that courage creates. Just the moment you begin to swerve in your plan you begin to carry out another's thought, and not your own. You become the directed and not the director. You forsake the courage and resolution of your own mind, and you therefore lack the very forces that you need to sustain and carry out your work. Instead of being self-reliant you become timid, and this invites failure. When you permit yourself to be influenced from your plan by another, you are unable to judge as you should, because you have allowed another's influence to deprive you of your courage and determination without absorbing any of his in return, so you are in much the same predicament as you would be in if you turned over all your worldly possessions to another without getting value received.

Concentrate on just the opposite of fear, want, poverty, sickness, etc. Never doubt your own ability. You have plenty, *if you will just use it.* A great many men are failures because they doubt their own capacity. Instead of building up strong mental forces, which would be of the greatest use to them, their fear thoughts tear them down. Fear paralyzes energy. It keeps us from attracting the forces that make success. Fear is the worst enemy we have.

Few people really know that they can accomplish much. They desire the full extent of their powers, but alas, it is only occasionally that you find a man who is aware of the great possibilities within him. When you believe with all your mind and heart and soul that you can do something, you thereby develop the courage to steadily and confidently live up to that belief. You have now gone a long way towards accomplishing it. Strong courage eliminates the injurious and opposing forces by summoning their masters, the yet-stronger forces that will serve you.

Courage is yours for the asking. All you have to do is to believe in it, claim it, and use it. One man of courage can fire with his spirit a whole army of men, whether military or industrial, because courage, like cowardice, is contagious.

Concentrate on Wealth

It was never intended that man should be poor. When wealth is obtained under the proper conditions, it broadens the life. Everything has its value. Everything has a good use and a bad use. The forces of mind, like wealth, can be directed either for good or evil. A little rest will re-create forces. Too much rest degenerates into laziness, and brainless, dreamy longings.

So, the first step toward acquiring wealth is to surround yourself with helpful influences; to claim for yourself an environment of culture, place yourself in it, and be molded by its influences.

Wealth is usually the fruit of achievement. It is not, however, altogether the result of being industrious. Thousands of persons work hard who never grow wealthy. Others with much less effort acquire wealth. Seeing possibilities is another step toward acquiring wealth. A man may be as industrious as he can possibly be, but if he does not use his mental forces he will be a laborer, to be directed by the man who uses to good advantage his mental forces.

No one can become wealthy in an ordinary lifetime by mere savings from earnings. Many scrimp and economize all their lives; but by so doing waste all their vitality and energy. For example, I know a man who used to walk to work. It took him an hour to go and an hour to return. He could have taken a car and gone in twenty minutes. He saved ten cents a day, but wasted an hour and a half. It was not a very profitable investment, unless the time spent in physical exercise yielded him large returns in the way of health.

The same amount of time spent in concentrated effort to overcome his unfavorable business environment might have firmly planted his feet in the path of prosperity.

One of the big mistakes made by many people is that they associate with those who fail to call out or develop the best that is in them. When the social side of life is developed too exclusively, and recreation or entertainment becomes the leading motive of a person's life, he acquires habits of extravagance instead of economy; habits of wasting his resources, physical, mental, moral, and spiritual, instead of conserving them.

The other day I attended a lecture on Prosperity. I knew the lecturer had been practically broke for ten years. I wanted to hear what he had to say. He spoke very well. He no doubt benefited some of his hearers, but he had not profited by his own teachings. I introduced myself and asked him if he believed in his maxims. He said he did. I asked him if they had made him prosperous. He said not exactly. I asked him why. He answered that he thought he was fated not to experience prosperity.

In half an hour, I showed that man why poverty had always been his companion. He had dressed poorly. He held his lectures in poor surroundings. By his actions and beliefs he attracted poverty. He did not realize that his thoughts and his surroundings exercised an unfavorable influence. I said: "Thoughts are moving forces; great powers. Thoughts of wealth attract wealth. Therefore, if you desire wealth you must attract the forces that will help you to secure it. Your thoughts attract a similar kind of thoughts. If you hold thoughts of poverty you attract poverty. If you make up your mind you are going to be wealthy, you will instill this thought into all your mental forces, and you will at the same time use every external condition to help you."

Business success depends on foresight, good judgment, grit, firm resolution, and settled purpose. But never forget that thought is as real a force as electricity. Let your thoughts be such that you will send out as good as you receive; if you do not, you are not enriching others, and therefore deserve not to be enriched.

Again I repeat that the first as well as the last step in acquiring wealth is to surround yourself with good influences—good thought, good health, good home and business environment, and successful business associates. Cultivate, by every legitimate means, the acquaintance of men of big caliber. Bring your thought vibrations in regard to business into harmony with theirs. This will make your society not only agreeable, but sought after, and, when you have formed intimate friendships with clean, reputable men of wealth, entrust to them, for investment, your surplus earnings, however small, until you have developed the initiative and business acumen to successfully manage your own investments. By this time you will, through such associations, have found your place in life which, if you have rightly concentrated upon and used your opportunities, will not be among men of small parts.

There is somewhere in every brain the energy that will get you out of that rut and put you far up on the mountain of success, if you can only use the energy. And hope, self-confidence, and the determination to do something supply the spark that makes the energy work.

You Can Concentrate, But Will You?

All have the ability to concentrate, but will you? You can, but whether you will or not depends on you. It is one thing to be able to do something, another to do it. There is far more ability not used than is used. Why do not more men of ability make something of themselves? There are comparatively few successful men, but many ambitious ones. Why do not more get along? Cases may differ, but the fault is usually their own. They have had chances, perhaps better ones than some others that have made good.

What would you like to do that you are not doing? If you think you should be "getting on" better, why don't you? Study yourself carefully. Learn your shortcomings. Sometimes only a mere trifle keeps one from branching out and becoming a success. Discover why you have not been making good—the cause of your failure. Have you been expecting someone to lead you, or to make a way for you? If you have, concentrate on a new line of thought.

There are two things absolutely necessary for success—energy and the will to succeed. Nothing can take the place of either of these.

When we see those with handicaps amounting to something great in the world, the able-bodied man should feel ashamed of himself if he does not make good. There is nothing that can resist the force of perseverance. The way ahead for all of us is not clear sailing, but all hard passages can be bridged.

Many men will not begin an undertaking unless they feel sure they will succeed in it. What a mistake! This would be right, if we were sure of what we could and could not do. But who knows? *There may be an obstruction there now that might not be there next week. There may not be an obstruction there now that will be there next week.* The trouble with most people is that just as soon as they see their way blocked they lose courage. They forget that usually there is a way around the difficulty. It's up to you to find it. If you tackle something with little effort, when the conditions call for a big effort, you will, of course, not win. Tackle everything with a feeling that you will use all the power within you to make it a success. This is the kind of concentrated effort that succeeds.

Most people are beaten before they start. They think they are going to encounter obstacles, and they look for them instead of for means to overcome them. The result is that they increase their obstacles instead of diminishing them. Have you ever undertaken something that you thought would be hard, but afterwards found it easy? That is the way a great many times. Things that look difficult in advance turn out to be easy of conquest when once encountered. So start out on your journey with the idea that the road is going to be clear for you, and that if it is not you will clear the way.

The one great keynote of success is to do whatever you have decided on. Don't be turned from your path, but resolve that you are going to accomplish what you set out to do. Don't be frightened at a few rebuffs, for they cannot stop the man that is determined—the man that knows in his heart that success is only bought by tremendous resolution, by concentrated and whole-hearted effort.

It is not so much skill that wins victories, as it is activity and great determination. There is no such thing as failure for the man who does his best. No matter what you may be working at, don't let this make you lose courage. *The tides are continually changing, and to-*

morrow or some other day they will turn to your advantage if you are a willing and ambitious worker. There is nothing that develops you and increases your courage like work. If it were not for work how monotonous life would become!

So I say to the man who wants to advance: "Don't look upon your present position as your permanent one. Keep your eyes open, and add those qualities to your makeup that will assist you when your opportunity comes. Be ever alert and on the watch for opportunities. Remember, we attract what we set our minds on. If we look for opportunities, we find them."

The Art of Concentration with Practical Exercises

Select some thought, and see how long you can hold your mind on it. It is well to have a clock at first and keep track of the time. If you decide to think about health, you can get a great deal of good from your thinking besides developing concentration. Think of health as being the greatest blessing in the world. Don't let any other thought drift in. The moment one starts to obtrude, make it get out.

Make it a daily habit of concentrating on this thought for, say, ten minutes. Practice until you can hold it to the exclusion of everything else. You will find it of the greatest value to centralize your thoughts on health. Regardless of your present condition, see yourself as you would like to be, and be blind to everything else. You will find it hard at first to forget your ailments, if you have any, but after a short while you can shut out these negative thoughts and see yourself as you want to be. Each time you concentrate, you form a more perfect image of health, and, as you come into its realization, you become healthy, strong, and wholesome.

I want to impress upon your mind that the habit of forming mental images is of the greatest value. It has always been used by successful men of all ages, but few realize its full importance.

Do you know that you are continually acting according to the images you form? If you allow yourself to mold negative images, you unconsciously build a negative disposition. You will think of poverty, weakness, disease, fear, etc., just as surely as you think of these will your objective life express itself in a like way. Just what we think, we will manifest in the external world.

In deep concentration you become linked with the great creative spirit of the universe, and the creative energy then flows through you, vitalizing your creations into form. In deep concentration your mind becomes attuned with the infinite and registers the cosmic intelligence and receives its messages. You become so full of the cosmic energy that you are flooded with divine power. This is a most desired state. It is then we realize the advantages of being connected with the supra-consciousness. The supra-consciousness registers the higher cosmic vibrations. It is often referred to as the wireless station, the message recorded coming from the universal mind.

Watch yourself during the day and see that your muscles do not become tense or strained. See how easy and relaxed you can keep yourself. See how poised you can be at all times. Cultivate a self-poised manner, instead of a nervous, strained appearance. This mental feeling will improve your carriage and demeanor. Stop all useless gestures and movements of the body. These mean that you have not proper control over your body. After you have acquired this control, notice how "ill-at-ease" people are that have not gained this control.

Get rid of any habit you have of twitching or jerking any part of your body. You will find that you make many involuntary movements. You can quickly stop any of these by merely centering your attention on the thought: "I will not."

No matter what you may be doing, imagine that it is your chief object in life. Imagine you are not interested in anything else in the world but what you are doing. Do not let your attention get away from the work you are at. Your attention will no doubt be rebellious, but control it, and do not let it control you.

When once you conquer the rebellious attention, you have achieved a greater victory than you can realize at the time.

By concentration you can control your temper. If you are one of those that flare up at the slightest "provocation" and never try to control yourself, just think this over a minute. Does it do you any good? Do you gain anything by it? Doesn't it put you out of poise for some time? Don't you know that this grows on you, and will eventually make you despised by all that have any dealings with you?

Many of you that read this may think you are not guilty of either of these faults, but if you will carefully watch yourself, you will probably find that you are, and, if so, you will be greatly helped by repeating this affirmation each morning:

"I am going to try today not to make a useless gesture or to worry over trifles, or become nervous or irritable. I intend to be calm, and, no difference what may be the circumstances, I will control myself. Henceforth, I resolve to be free from all signs that show lack of self-control."

Now, a word on needless talking. It seems natural to want to tell others what you know; but, by learning to control these desires, you can wonderfully strengthen your powers of concentration. Remember, you have all you can do to attend to your own business. Do not waste your time in thinking of others, or in gossiping about them.

If, from your own observation, you learn something about another person that is detrimental, keep it to yourself. Your opinion may afterwards turn out to be wrong anyway; but whether right or wrong, you have strengthened your will by controlling your desire to communicate your views.

If you hear good news, resist the desire to tell it to the first person you meet and you will be benefited thereby. It will require the concentration of all your powers of resistance to prohibit the desire to tell. After you feel that you have complete control over your desires, you can then tell your news. But you must be able to suppress the desire to communicate the news until you are fully ready to tell it. Persons that do not possess this power of control over desires are apt to tell things that they should not, thereby often involving both themselves and others in needless trouble.

If you are in the habit of getting excited when you hear unpleasant news, just control yourself and receive it without any exclamation of surprise. Say to yourself, "Nothing is going to cause me to lose my self-control." You will find from experience that this self-control will be worth much to you in business. You will be looked upon as a cool-headed businessman, and this in time becomes a valuable asset. Of course, circumstances alter cases. At times it is necessary to become enthused. But be ever on the lookout for opportunities for the practice of self-control. "He that ruleth his spirit is greater than he that ruleth a city."

Concentrate So You Will Not Forget

We remember only that which makes a deep impression; hence we must first deepen our impressions by associating in our minds certain ideas that are related to them.

Let's say a wife gives her husband a letter to mail. He does not think about it, but automatically puts it in his pocket and forgets all about it. When the letter was given to him had he said to himself, "I will mail this letter. The box is at the next corner and when I pass it I must drop this letter," it would have enabled him to recall the letter the instant he reached the mailbox.

The same rule holds good in regard to more important things. For example, if you are instructed to drop in and see Mr. Smith while out to lunch today, you will not forget it, if, at the moment the instruction is given, you say to yourself something similar to this: "When I get to the corner of Blank Street, on my way to lunch, I shall turn to the right and call on Mr. Smith." In this way the impression is made, the connection established, and the sight of the associated object recalls the errand.

The important thing to do is to deepen the impression at the very moment it enters your mind. This is made possible not only by concentrating the mind upon the idea itself, but by surrounding it with all possible association of ideas, so that each one will reinforce the others.

The mind is governed by laws of association, such as the law that ideas that enter the mind at the same time emerge at the same time, one assisting in recalling the others. You can train yourself to remember in this way by the concentration of the attention on your purpose, in accordance with the laws of association.

How Concentration Can Fulfill Your Desire

It is a spiritual law that the desire to do necessarily implies the ability to do."

All natural desires can be realized. It would be wrong for the Infinite to create wants that could not be supplied. Man's very soul is in his power to think, and it, therefore, is the essence of all created things. Every instinct of man leads to thought, and in every thought there is great possibility because true thought development, when allied to those mysterious powers which perhaps transcend it, has been the cause of all the world's true progress.

Silent, concentrated thought is more potent than spoken words, for speech distracts from the focusing power of the mind by drawing more and more attention to the without.

Man must learn more and more to depend on himself; to seek more for the Infinite within. It is from this source alone that he gains the power to solve his practical difficulties. No one should give up when there is always the resources of Infinity. The cause of failure is that men search in the wrong direction for success, because they are not conscious of their real powers, which when used are capable of guiding them.

The Infinite within is foreign to those who go through life without developing their spiritual powers. But the Infinite helps only he who helps himself. There is no such thing as a Special "Providence." Man will not receive help from the Infinite except to the extent that he believes and hopes and prays for help from this great source.

Remember that the first step in concentration is to form a Mental Image of what you wish to accomplish. This image becomes a thought-seed that attracts thoughts of a similar nature. Around this thought, when it is once planted in the imagination or creative region of the mind, you group or build associated thoughts, which continue to grow as long as your desire is keen enough to compel close concentration.

Form the habit of thinking of something you wish to accomplish for five minutes each day. Shut every other thought out of consciousness. Be confident that you will succeed; make up your mind that all obstacles will be overcome, and that you can rise above any environment.

A great aid in the development of concentration is to write out your thoughts on that which lies nearest your heart and to continue, little by little, to add to it until you have as nearly as possible exhausted the subject. You will find that each day as you focus your forces on this thought at the center of the stream of consciousness, new plans, ideas, and methods will flash into your mind.

We can attract those things that will help us. Very often we seem to receive help in a miraculous way. It may be slow in coming, but once the silent unseen forces are put into operation, they will bring results so long as we do our part. By forming a strong mental image of your desire, you plant the thought-seed that begins working in your interest and, in time, that desire, if in harmony with your higher nature, will materialize.

It may seem that it would be unnecessary to caution you to concentrate only upon achievement that will be good for you, and work no harm to another, but there are many who forget others and their rights, in their anxiety to achieve success. All good things are possible for you to have, but only as you bring your forces into harmony with that law that requires that we mete out justice to fellow travelers as we journey along life's road. So first think over the thing wanted and if it would be good for you to have. Say: "I want to do this; I am going to work to secure it. The way will be open for me."

If you fully grasp mentally the thought of success and hold it in mind each day, you gradually make a pattern or mold, which in time will materialize. But by all means keep free from doubt and fear, the destructive forces. Never allow these to become associated with your thoughts.

At last you will create the desired conditions, and receive help in many unlooked-for ways that will lift you out of the undesired environment. Life will then seem very different to you, for you will have found happiness through awakening within yourself the power to become the master of circumstances, instead of their slave.

Remember the mystical words of Jesus, the Master: "Whatsoever thing ye desire when ye pray, pray as if ye had already received and ye shall have."

Ideals Developed by Concentration

We often hear people spoken of as idealists. The fact is we are all idealists to a certain extent, and upon the ideals we picture depend our ultimate success. You must have the mental image if you are to produce the material thing. Everything is first created in the mind. When you control your thoughts, you become a creator. You receive divine ideas and shape them to your individual needs. All things of this world are to you just what you think they are. Your happiness and success depend upon your ideals.

Concentrate Upon Your Ideals and They Will Become Material Actualities. Through concentration we work out our ideals in physical life. Your future depends upon the ideals you are forming now. Your past ideals are determining your present. Therefore, if you want a bright future, you must begin to prepare for it today.

We say that a man is as changeable as the weather. What is meant is his ideals change. Every time you change your ideal you think differently. You become like a rudderless boat on an ocean. Therefore realize the importance of holding to your ideal until it becomes a reality.

You get up in the morning determined that nothing will make you lose your temper. This is your ideal of a person of real strength and poise. Something takes place that upsets you completely, and you lose your temper. For the time being you forget your ideal. If you had just thought a second of what a well-poised person implies you would not have become angry. *You lose your poise when you forget your ideal.* Each time we allow our ideals to be shattered we also weaken our willpower. Holding to your ideals develops willpower. Never forget this.

Why do so many fail? Because they don't hold to their ideal until it becomes a mental habit. When they concentrate on it to the exclusion of all other things, it becomes a reality. "I am that which I think myself to be."

You must give some hours to concentrated, consistent, persistent thought. You must study yourself and your weaknesses.

No man gets over a fence by wishing himself on the other side. He must climb.

No man gets out of the rut of dull, tiresome, monotonous life by merely wishing himself out of the rut. He must climb.

If you are standing still, or going backward, there is something wrong. You are the person to find out what is wrong.

Don't think that you are neglected, or not understood, or not appreciated.

Such thoughts are the thoughts of failure.

You know that the only thing in the world that you have got to count upon is yourself.

Concentration Reviewed

In this closing chapter, I want to impress you to concentrate on what you do, instead of performing most of your work unconsciously or automatically, until you have formed habits that give you the mastery of your work, and your life powers and forces.

Very often the hardest part of work is thinking about it. When you get right into it, it does not seem so disagreeable. This is the experience of many when they first commence to learn how to concentrate. So never think it a difficult task, but undertake it with the "I Will Spirit," and you will find that its acquirement will be as easy as its application will be useful.

Read the life of any great man, and you will generally find that the dominant quality that made him successful was the ability to concentrate. Study those who have been failures, and you will often find that lack of concentration was the cause.

Never say, "I can't concentrate today." You can do it just the minute you say, "I will." You *can* keep your thoughts from straying, just the same as you can control your arms. Once you realize this fact, you can train the will to concentrate on anything you wish. If it wanders, it is your fault. You are not using your will. But don't blame it on your will, and say it is weak. The will is the same whether you act as if it were weak or as if it were strong. When you act as if your will is strong you say, "I can." When you act as if it were weak you say, "I can't." It requires the same amount of effort.

Some men get in the habit of thinking, "I can't," and they fail. Others think, "I can," and succeed. So remember, it is for you to decide whether you will join the army of "I can't" or "I can."

The big mistake with so many is that they don't realize that when they say, "I can't," they really say, "I won't try." You cannot tell what you can do until you try. "Can't" means you will not try.

Before going to bed tonight, repeat: "I am going to choose my own thoughts, and to hold them as long as I choose. I am going to shut out all thoughts that weaken or interfere, that make me timid. My Will is as strong as anyone else's." While going to work the next morning, repeat this Keep this up for a month, and you will find you will have a better opinion of yourself. These are the factors that make you a success. Hold fast to them always.

Concentration is nothing but willing to do a certain thing. All foreign thoughts can be kept out by willing that they stay out. You cannot realize your possibilities until you commence to direct your mind.

You have at times been in a position that required courage, and you were surprised at the amount you showed. Now, when once you arouse yourself, you have this courage all the time and it is not necessary to have a special occasion reveal it. My object in so strongly impressing this on your mind is to make you aware that the same courage, the same determination that you show at certain exceptionable times, you have at your command at all times. It is a part of your vast resources. Use it often and well, in working out the highest destiny of which you are capable.

Father Time keeps going on and on. Every day he rolls around means one less day for you on this planet. Most of us only try to master the external conditions of this world. We think our success and happiness depend on us doing so. These are, of course, important, and I don't want you to think they are not; but I want you to realize that when death comes, only those inherent and acquired qualities and conditions within the mentality—your character, conduct, and soul growth—will go with you. If these are what they should be, you need not be afraid of not being successful and happy, for with these qualities you can mold external materials and conditions.

Now start from this minute to act according to the advice of the higher self in everything you do. If you do, its ever-harmonious forces will necessarily ensure a successful fulfillment of all your life purposes. Whenever you feel tempted to disobey your higher promptings, hold the thought: "My-higher-self-ensures-to-me-the-happiness-of-doing-that-which-best-answers-my-true-relations-to-all-others."

You possess latent talents, which when developed and used are of assistance to you and others. But if you do not properly use them, you shirk your duty, and you will be the loser and suffer from the consequences. Others will also be worse off if you do not fulfill your obligations.

Hold the thought: "I-will-live-for-my-best. I-seek-wisdom, self-knowledge, happiness-and-power-to-help-others. I-act-from-the-higher-self, therefore-only-the-best-can-come-to-me."

The more we become conscious of the presence of the higher self, the more we should try to become a true representative of the human soul in all its wholeness and holiness, instead of wasting our time dwelling on some trifling external quality or defect. We should try to secure a true conception of what we really are so as not to over value the external furnishings. You will then not surrender your dignity or self-respect when others ignorantly make a display of material things to show off. Only the person who realizes that he is a permanent Being knows what the true self is

"Theron Q. Dumont" was one of several pseudonyms used by WILLIAM WALKER ATKINSON, a popular and innovative New Thought writer and publisher in the early twentieth century. Born in Baltimore, Maryland, in 1862, Atkinson became a successful attorney in 1894. Following a series of illnesses, he immersed himself in New Thought literature. He soon became an important figure in the early days of the movement, publishing magazines such as *Suggestion, New Thought,* and *Advanced Thought.* Under the aegis of his own publishing company, Yogi Publication Society, Atkinson wrote many self-bylined works, and many titles under the pseudonyms Yogi Ramacharaka, Magus Incognito, Theron Q. Dumont, and Three Initiates. Under the last of these, Atkinson wrote his most popular and enduring work, *The Kybalion.* Published in 1908 by Atkinson's Chicago-based press, *The Kybalion* is perhaps the most widely read occult book of the twentieth century. Atkinson died in California in 1932.

MITCH HOROWITZ, who abridged and introduced this volume, is the PEN Award-winning author of books including *Occult America* and *The Miracle Club: How Thoughts Become Reality. The Washington Post* says Mitch "treats esoteric ideas and movements with an even-handed intellectual studiousness that is too often lost in today's raised-voice discussions." Follow him @MitchHorowitz.